Occupational Therapy

Activities for Kids

Occupational Therapy
Activities for Kids

100 Fun Games and Exercises to Build Skills

Heather Ajzenman, OTD, OTR/L, HPCS

Illustrations by Siiri Väisänen

ROCKRIDGE PRESS

For general information on our other products and services or to obtain technical support, please contact our Customer Care Department within the United States at (866) 744-2665, or outside the United States at (510) 253-0500.

Rockridge Press publishes its books in a variety of electronic and print formats. Some content that appears in print may not be available in electronic books, and vice versa.

Interior & Cover Designer: Suzanne LaGasa
Art Producer: Maura Boland
Editor: Lauren O'Neal
Production Editor: Nora Milman

Illustration © 2019 Siiri Väisänene

ISBN: Print 978-1-64611-076-6 | eBook 978-1-64611-077-3

R0

To my daughter, Sophiya Lily, who allowed me to type this book one-handed as she snuggled on me as a newborn, and to my husband, Andrei, who provided incredible support throughout the process.

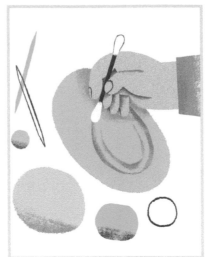

SKILLS LEARNED

Attention

Interoception

Sight

Communication

Memory

Smell

Emotional Regulation

Oral Motor Skills

Social Relationships

Fine Motor Skills

Planning and Problem-Solving

Taste

Gross Motor Skills

Play Development

Touch

Hand-Eye Coordination

Proprioception

Vestibular

Hearing

Self-Awareness

Visual Spatial Skills

Shared Engagement

Chapter One

All About Occupational Therapy for Kids

BEFORE WE JUMP INTO 100 FUN activities to support and enhance your child's skills, let's explore the value of occupational therapy and the benefits it can provide children of all different abilities. This chapter covers the occupational therapy process, the settings where services are typically offered, strategies for modifying activities, ideas for toys and objects to use, and further explanations of various diagnoses and differences that can benefit from occupational therapy.

What Is Occupational Therapy?

Occupational therapy is the use of meaningful activities to help individuals develop, regain, or adapt skills to participate in daily routines. The kinds of activities that make up a daily routine are referred to as "occupations"—not to be confused with professions or careers. Typical occupations include sleep, play and leisure, work, and self-care (such as dressing, bathing, and feeding). Occupational therapists work with people of all ages, including children and adults with developmental disabilities, physical injuries, neurological conditions, and mental health conditions.

These occupations have always been central to human development, but the field of occupational therapy wasn't recognized until the early 1900s, when the organization now known as the American Occupational Therapy Association (AOTA) was founded. Its initial focus was medical, but the profession has expanded to address people's social needs as well.

Children's primary occupation is play, so occupational therapists help children and families engage in individually tailored, play-focused activities to work toward specific developmental goals based on the child's needs, family routines, and other influences.

The Value of Play

As the primary occupation of childhood, play is a lot more than just fun and games! It's also the foundation for overall development, health, and well-being. Play development begins at birth, when children first engage in sensorimotor play while exploring their environment and interacting with objects and people. Play impacts gross and fine motor development and sensory processing, as children learn to use their large muscles to gain strength, body awareness, and coordination; their hands to manipulate and access materials; and their senses to engage with the world around them. Play has a huge role in social and emotional development, providing opportunities to regulate and express complex emotions, engage with and relate to others, and learn to communicate effectively. It also helps kids develop higher-level skills such as abstract and logical sequential thinking, open-mindedness, and executive-functioning skills, which set the stage for academic learning.

Children with disabilities often face challenges during play due to their differences, which may be physiological, social-emotional, sensory, and/or cognitive. These challenges affect how they come up with play ideas, communicate thoughts, and express emotions. Occupational therapists observe and analyze how a child plays to understand their abilities, then work with the child and family to build skills and improve participation.

For kids to benefit from occupational therapy, the activities must be meaningful to them. If your child loves dinosaurs, for example, you might create a dinosaur-hunt obstacle course to help them work on gross motor skills or have them color a dinosaur picture to work on fine motor skills.

Is Occupational Therapy Right for My Child?

Does your child have difficulty getting dressed, eating meals, writing with a pencil, throwing and catching a ball, remaining calm during changes in routines, reacting to different sounds or textures, playing with peers, staying balanced on the playground, keeping their space organized, or paying attention during school? Occupational therapy can help children with all these skills and more, so they can be as independent and successful as possible when playing, socializing, learning, and completing daily routines.

A doctor or teacher might recommend occupational therapy services for your child based on any number of challenges. Regardless of why your child qualifies for it, occupational therapy offers a great opportunity to help children and families develop new skills and increase participation in fun, meaningful, and essential daily activities.

In 1975, the Individuals with Disabilities Education Act legally required schools to provide free and appropriate public education to children with disabilities, including access to therapy. In 2004, that expanded to include students with any learning needs, which increased opportunities for occupational therapy services in schools.

Which Kids Can Benefit from Occupational Therapy?

All children can benefit from learning strategies for taking part in everyday routines. That said, let's take a look at some common diagnoses, the challenges they present, and activities that children can engage in to improve performance and successfully participate in daily activities. Many of these developmental differences have overlapping as well as unique needs; for example, children with sensory processing disorder and autism spectrum disorder may have similar sensory challenges, but some of their other needs will be completely different. Parents and caregivers should consider what applies to their child.

SENSORY PROCESSING DISORDER (SPD)

Sensory processing is how the body takes in, interprets, and responds to sensory information. Humans have eight unique senses. You've probably heard of the first five: visual (sight), auditory (hearing), tactile (touch), olfactory (smell), and gustatory (taste). But there are also three more: proprioception (your sense of body positioning and movement in relationship to your environment), vestibular (your sense of balance and movement in relationship to the position of your head), and interoception (your sense of internal body parts and emotions, such as differentiating between hunger, pain, and butterflies in your stomach).

Children with SPD have difficulties with one or more of their senses. They might become overstimulated easily or, conversely, constantly seek more sensory stimulation. They might take a long time to respond to certain sensory information, or not recognize it at all. They might use too little or too much force on items, misinterpret social cues, struggle with regulating emotions, or face challenges with eating and other self-care tasks.

Occupational therapists can help children improve their sensory processing by using play to help them explore their senses, especially in relationship to their daily routines. They can also help families do things like modify their home to accommodate a child's sensory needs.

AUTISM SPECTRUM DISORDER (ASD)

Autism spectrum disorder (ASD) is a developmental disability that impacts how people perceive their surroundings and interact with others. Differences include challenges with verbal and nonverbal communication, difficulties with social interactions, highly preferred interests, preference for structured routines, and sensory processing challenges. ASD is wide-ranging and unique to the individual.

Occupational therapists can help identify which skills need development. They might use sensory approaches, modify overwhelming activities, provide meaningful social engagement through play, offer opportunities for different types of communication, and use visuals to assist with routines and learning.

ATTENTION DEFICIT HYPERACTIVITY DISORDER (ADHD)

Attention deficit hyperactivity disorder (ADHD) is characterized by inattention, hyperactivity, and impulsivity. Kids with ADHD often exhibit difficulties with executive functioning, which is involved in tasks like planning, organizing ideas, problem-solving, and regulating emotions.

Occupational therapy activities for children with ADHD may include designing and completing multi-step obstacle courses to work on attention and problem-solving, creating schedules to complete morning routines, or engaging in physical activities before switching to seated activities to improve attention.

CEREBRAL PALSY AND OTHER NEUROLOGICAL DIAGNOSES

Cerebral palsy is a movement disorder resulting from damage to the brain before or shortly after birth. Symptoms include floppy or rigid muscles, involuntary movement, atypical body positioning, coordination impairments, and difficulties walking. Movement impairments may affect just the legs, but can also affect the torso, arms, hands, head, speech, vision, and cognitive abilities. Other neurological diagnoses that can have similar symptoms include traumatic brain injuries, viral infections impacting the brain and spine, and seizure disorders.

Occupational therapists can help children position themselves in a way that lets them actively engage in play and self-care, teach them how to use wheelchairs to move around, and work on developing hand skills with them.

DOWN SYNDROME AND OTHER GENETIC DISORDERS

One of the most common genetic disorders that causes developmental differences in children is Down syndrome. Caused by an extra partial or full copy of chromosome 21, it leads to differences in physical development and learning, such as low muscle tone, communication difficulties, and challenges with short- and long-term memory. Associated health issues may include heart deficits, gastrointestinal challenges, immune disorders, spinal instability, and sleeping challenges.

Among other things, occupational therapy can help kids with Down syndrome develop gross, fine, and oral motor skills so they can do things like zip a coat, cut with scissors, and successfully chew food.

OTHER DEVELOPMENTAL DIFFERENCES

Sometimes children arrive at developmental milestones later than expected, or don't meet them at all. These children may appear clumsy, have difficulty with activities like buttoning and handwriting, or have trouble processing verbal directions. They may also experience heightened stress and anxiety, have difficulty communicating their needs, or become upset easily.

Occupational therapy can help these kids with activities to meet their needs, such as obstacle courses to build strength, visual scanning tasks to decrease clumsiness, or manipulation activities to build fine motor strength. Adaptations may include simplifying written work during handwriting, providing visuals for following directions, or teaching kids how to recognize physical responses to various emotions.

ANY KID CAN BENEFIT!

Though occupational therapy is intended for children with differences that impact their daily lives, the activities in this book can help any kid strengthen certain areas, develop skills, or learn new tools and strategies for improving motor, sensory processing, social-emotional, visual, and cognitive abilities.

How Does the Occupational Therapy Process Work?

Occupational therapy services can take place anywhere—at home, at school, in a therapy clinic or hospital, or in the community. For children under age 3, the most natural environment is typically the home, and the therapist helps create an individualized family service plan (IFSP) to develop family-centered goals for specific developmental needs. Children over age 3 get an individualized education plan (IEP) if their developmental differences affect learning, and they can receive occupational therapy services in integrated classrooms, special-needs classrooms, small groups, or individually. Some children need modifications, such as extra time for tests or voice software to help them type. In these instances, a 504 plan can be established to let children fully integrate within their learning environment.

Outside school, many children receive outpatient occupational therapy in private clinics, in hospitals, on the playground, in the pool, or even on a horse. This route may require a referral from your primary care provider. The process typically involves an initial evaluation, which includes parent/caregiver interviews, clinical observations, and standardized testing. The therapist will set goals based on your child's needs and work on them during each session using child-centered, play-based activities to improve the child's engagement with daily life tasks. These services are typically billed to insurance, but some families pay out of pocket or submit for reimbursement if they're not covered. Length and number of sessions vary based on insurance, scheduling, and the child's needs, but typically children receive one or two 30- to 60-minute sessions per week.

The activities provided in this book are a great resource to complement what your child may be working on with an occupational therapist and can help you get creative when working on these goals at home.

CHOOSING THE RIGHT TOYS FOR YOUR CHILD

When choosing toys for your child, consider cost, durability, and the number of toys available at a time (too many can make it hard for your child to pay attention fully). Here are some other factors to take into account, depending on your child's needs:

- **Age appropriateness** Children under the age of 1 benefit from toys that they can reach for, grasp, and safely explore with their hands and mouth. Between ages 1 and 2, children begin to learn cause and effect, enjoying toys they can stack, sort, or simply act on, such as by pressing a button to make a light or noise. Between ages 2 and 3, children show interest in building, coloring, pretend play, and rough-and-tumble gross motor activities. From ages 3 to 6, children expand play with imaginary concepts and rules.

- **Ease of access** Explore toys that can be used in different positions to build strength or reduce challenges presented by motor, sensory, or cognitive issues.

- **Ease of use** Does the toy encourage use of both hands? Are there small items or parts to help your child work on fine motor skills? If small components are too difficult for your child, consider toys with larger pieces.

- **Sensory aspects** Colors, flashing lights, and sounds can attract a child to work on specific developmental needs, or they might be overstimulating. Various textures (bumpy, sticky, etc.) can help a child increase their tolerance but can also lead to large negative emotional responses.

- **Simplicity** "Open-ended" toys that can be used in more than one way encourage children to think creatively.

- **Social aspects** Consider toys and activities that promote sharing ideas, working together, and compromising as part of play.

What Materials Will I Need?

Each activity in the book includes a list of materials you'll need. Most will be everyday items such as arts and crafts supplies (paper, markers, glue, etc.), miscellaneous household items (cardboard boxes, laundry baskets, etc.), and toys (your child's preferred toys as well as common play items like play dough).

A few activities also call for some specialized materials, but whenever possible I've provided ideas for substitutions or instructions on how to make your own. These include:

- **Balance board** An unsteady surface for your child to stand on so they can work on balance, coordination, and staying calm with both feet off the floor (see page 75 to make your own).

- **Body sock** A large Lycra "sock" your child can put their entire body in. The tight, stretchy material provides resistance so your child can do heavy work as they move their body inside the sock, as well as deep pressure to help them calm their body and regulate their emotions.

- **Crash mat** A large, cushioned mat for your child to safely jump or crash into. It can also be used for lounging or providing additional deep pressure (see page 27 to make your own).

- **Exercise ball** Also known as a therapy or yoga ball, this is a large ball your child can sit on to develop muscle strength, balance, and coordination.

- **Hoberman sphere** A toy that looks kind of like a many-jointed geodesic sphere, capable of folding into a smaller size and stretching out to a larger size. It's great for helping children synchronize their breath and calm their body.

- **Water table** A plastic play table with high sides that can be filled with water and water toys.

Tips and Tricks

If your child is in occupational therapy, talk to your provider about creating a complementary program at home. Here are some suggestions for using the activities in this book as part of that program:

- Incorporate one or two activities each day that are relevant to your child's needs. Introduce them slowly, starting with one activity every other day and working up to daily activities.

- Pay attention to your child's cues. Have they had a long week? Are they fatigued? Don't push them to do activities. Instead, find things that might help calm their body, such as some of the sensory processing strategies in chapter 2.

- Your child will get the most out of "just right" activities. "Just right" activities are developmentally appropriate, consider the child's strengths and weaknesses, aren't too easy or too hard for the child's current abilities, and are engaging and meaningful.

- If you need to modify the activity for your child, go ahead! Most of the activities include suggestions on how to make them easier or harder.

- Consider your own needs. For example, if you don't want messy activities in the house, take them outside, or if your own sensory system doesn't tolerate certain textures, feel free to modify the materials.

Chapter Two

Sensory Processing Skills

HUMANS HAVE EIGHT SENSES: SIGHT, HEARING, touch, smell, taste, proprioception (sense of body positioning and movement in relation to the environment around you), vestibular (sense of balance and movement in relation to your head), and interoception (sense of internal body parts and emotions). Children with sensory processing challenges have trouble taking in information from these senses and figuring out what it means. If your child has autism spectrum disorder, sensory processing disorder, or similar conditions, you may notice them becoming overstimulated and withdrawing, seeking sensory input and getting overexcited, and/or taking a long time to respond to sensory information. The activities in this chapter will help your child explore their senses—but observe their responses carefully. Stop if they become overwhelmed, and avoid things they have aversions to. It's okay if they're hesitant, but don't force them to do anything if they become upset or have big feelings.

Stuck in the Mud

Here's a safe and fun way to increase your child's comfort with different food textures and perhaps even tastes. Start with a food that your child likes and gradually expand to similar items before introducing something completely new.

Age: 1+

Prep time: 10 minutes

Activity time: 15 minutes

MATERIALS

Place mat (optional)

Bib or smock (optional)

Gooey food such as applesauce, hummus, pudding, whipped cream

Small toy cars, animal figures, or any items that can get dirty

Foods for dipping, such as fruit slices, pretzels, etc.

Paper towels or wet cloth

STEPS

1. Use a clean surface such as a table or high chair with tray. Put down the place mat (if using). Have your child wear a bib or smock if they'll tolerate it.

2. Spread the gooey food on the table or place mat and invite your child to explore it using the toys and/or their fingers.

3. Encourage your child and talk about how touching these items feels. Stop the activity if your child feels overwhelmed.

4. Introduce other food items that can be dipped, letting your child freely explore and come up with new play ideas.

5. If your child is comfortable, invite them to lick the dipped food or their fingers.

6. Offer paper towels or wet cloths as needed. If they want to wash their hands or stop playing, that's okay! Provide lots of positive praise for all attempts made.

To make it easier: *Have your child just look at the food and describe what it looks like.*

To make it harder: *Hide a pretzel stick in the "mud" and let your child find it!*

Match That Sound!

What's that noise? Practice attention and listening skills by matching items based only on their sounds.

Age: 1+

Prep time: 5 minutes

Activity time: 10 minutes

MATERIALS

10 plastic eggs or other empty containers

2 each of 5 different objects to make the sounds (e.g., 2 bells, 2 coins, 2 small rocks, etc.)

STEPS

1. Place each of the 10 objects in a separate container.

2. Without your child looking, mix them around.

3. Have your child pick up a container and shake it to hear the sound, then shake other containers to try to find the matching one.

To make it easier: *Reduce the number of matches to just 2 or 3.*

To make it harder: *Have your child guess which object is inside. Or, turn it into a visual and auditory matching memory game, placing each container back in the same location after picking up one that doesn't match. Try to match as many as possible based on location to win.*

3 … 2 … 1 … Blast Off!

Does your child need to "wake up" their body or find a way to help their body calm and get regulated? Make a fun game of blasting off to the moon with movements such as swinging, jumping, or crashing. Use this activity to help their body get "in the right zone" for play, learning, or daily routines.

Age: 1+
Prep time: 5 minutes
Activity time: 10 minutes

MATERIALS

Use one of the following materials or simply let your child use their body to provide the action.

Playground swing or baby bucket swing

Mini trampoline

Large crash mat or pillows (see page 27 to make your own)

Sit 'n Spin

STEPS

1. Set up the swing, trampoline, or other item, or simply prepare your child for different body positions, such as jumping or spinning.

2. Help your child onto the swing or other item, or prepare them to jump or spin.

3. Give blast off directions: "3 … 2 … 1 … blast off!" or "Ready … set … go!"

4. Have your child swing as high as they can, jump as high as they can, crash (if safe), or spin, changing directions as needed to avoid dizziness.

5. Use this activity in small amounts so it doesn't overstimulate your child.

To make it easier: *Follow up with proprioceptive activities if your child becomes overstimulated, such as Make Me a Sandwich! (page 33), big hugs, or deep squeezes.*

To make it harder: *If you have multiple options available, such as a swing and a trampoline, let your child choose. This helps them learn which activities are the most helpful to regulate their bodies.*

Sight	Hearing	Touch	Proprioception	Interoception	Emotional Regulation	SKILLS LEARNED

Sensory Safe Space/Hideout

Create a semi-permanent safe space with various sensory items to help your child calm down.

Age: 1+
Prep time: 30 minutes
Activity time: As long as needed to help your child's body calm

MATERIALS

Sheets to drape over a surface or a pop-up child's tent

Soft sheets, heavy/weighted blankets, pillows

Flashlight or dim light of choice

Calming music

Preferred tactile items, such as a squishy ball or soft stuffed animal

STEPS

Have your child help set up this space with you when happy and engaged. Work together to choose the location and decide what materials and objects to use.

1. Ideas for setup:

   * To create the safe space, drape the sheets over a bed frame or chair and a bookshelf, or use a pop-up tent.

   * Line the space with sheets, pillows, and blankets.

   * Place your lighting and music sources on a small side table in, or next to, the safe space.

   * Place a variety of tactile items within this space.

2. Talk with your child about the space, visit the space, discuss when they might want to go there (such as when they're upset or angry or when their body feels tired), and practice using the items.

3. Encourage your child to visit this space when experiencing big feelings. Show them how they can get under the pillows or wrap up in the blankets, using music or soft lights as needed.

Chew and Chill

Does your child tend to chew on clothing, put their hands in their mouth, or calm down when having a crunchy snack? Explore these options to learn how to help your child meet their oral motor needs and increase their interest in other activities.

Age: 1+
Prep time: 2 minutes
Activity time: As long as needed

MATERIALS

Use one or more of the following, depending on your child's preferences.

Chewy foods, such as dried fruit or beef jerky

Crunchy foods, such as oatmeal bars, graham crackers, or popcorn (for children 4 and older)

Gum (for children 4 and older)

Thick drinks with a straw, such as smoothies or applesauce

Items like a chewy tube or chewy necklace for longer chewing needs (optional)

STEPS

1. Observe when your child tends to put things in their mouth, chews clothing, or has a hard time keeping their body calm.

2. Test which snacks or chewy items help in these situations by providing different chewing options. If your child comes home dysregulated after a long day of "holding it together" at school, these snacks can be very helpful.

DIY No-Sew Crash Mat

Some kids need to jump, crash, and get full-body squeezes to make their bodies feel calm. A crash mat gives them a large, soft, safe surface to do just that! Make your own crash mat at a low cost with no sewing and you'll have a great tool to meet your child's physical needs.

Age: 1+
Prep time: 30 minutes
Activity time: As much as needed

MATERIALS

Pillows and/or body pillows

Duvet cover (button or zipper closure)

Duct tape (optional)

Duvet (optional)

Blankets, stuffed animals, beanbag chairs (optional)

STEPS

1. Start off by putting as many pillows and/or body pillows as needed into the duvet cover. If desired, duct tape larger pillows together to reduce shifting, and then pull the duvet cover over the pillows.

2. Use optional items such as a duvet, blankets, stuffed animals, or a beanbag chair to fill in the gaps.

3. Find a safe place and let your child jump and crash onto the mat, or let your child get under the mat on another soft surface to get full-body squeezes.

To make it harder: *Have your child help you make the crash mat. Pushing items into the duvet cover is a great heavy work activity, and finding the necessary items within your home is a good visual searching exercise.*

Sensory Diet

This is an activity for you, the parent/caregiver, that will help you design a "sensory diet" for your child. A sensory diet is a group of activities and sensory strategies you can schedule throughout your child's day to help them with sensory processing, emotional regulation, and attention. Each child is different, so observe to see which activities your child does and does not benefit from. For best results, work with your child's occupational therapist to create a tailored sensory diet.

Age: 1+
Prep time: Ongoing
Activity time: Ongoing

No materials are needed for this activity.

STEPS

1. Watch your child during the day and note which sensory activities they tend to:

   - Seek

   - Avoid

   - Have a hard time doing

   - Get overwhelmed by

2. Make note of when these events occur and how your child responds emotionally.

3. Explore *why* your child responds to certain sensory information. Ask yourself:

   - Does my child crash into things because they need more deep pressure input or lack awareness of their body while moving?

   - What is it about certain clothing textures that makes my child upset?

Ask your child why they're reacting this way—they may be able to explain it.

Ask your child's occupational therapist what a particular action or reaction might mean.

4. Try a variety of sensory approaches with support from your child's occupational therapist and activity suggestions in this book. For each sensory system, consider whether certain activities will either help your child regulate or heighten negative responses. What adaptations can you make to set your child up for success?

5. Continue to observe how your child participates in the different activities and their responses to various sensory tools. Modify as needed by adding, changing, or removing activities, depending on how they work.

Sensory Calming Bin

Create your child's own customized calming sensory bin containing all the sensory tools needed for your child to explore and use when they need to regulate their body and emotions.

Age: 1+
Prep time: 30 to 45 minutes
Activity time: As much as needed

MATERIALS

Sensory tools (e.g., noise-canceling headphones, weighted blanket, squishy toy, fidget toy, chewy tube, nonperishable crunchy snacks, play dough, soft stuffed animals, etc.)

A durable, portable box big enough to fit the sensory tools but small enough to take on the go

Markers, glitter paint, gems, etc., to decorate the box (optional)

Sensory Strategy Cards (page 52) (optional)

STEPS

1. Identify which sensory tools you need based on what sensory systems your child overresponds to and/or seeks out. For example, if your child is overstimulated by sound, consider noise-canceling headphones or earplugs. If your child craves tactile/feeling items, consider a squishy or fidget toy.

2. Fill the box with the appropriate items. Add or remove items over time as you figure out what works best for your child. Decorate the box if desired.

3. Add the Sensory Strategy Cards (if using) to help your child visualize activities they want to do, which can be helpful when a child finds it difficult to communicate.

4. Tell your child where you'll keep the box and let them know they can use it anywhere, anytime they get upset. Encourage your child to use the box the next time they feel dysregulated.

Safety tip: *Be mindful of small items for children under age 3.*

Light-Up Letters

It's going to get dark! Get out your flashlight and engage in a fun alphabet learning game to help your child work on attention, following directions, and using their visual sense for learning.

Age: 2+
Prep time: 15 minutes
Activity time: 20 minutes

MATERIALS

Flashlight

Magnetic letters

STEPS

1. In a dark room, with the lights off and the blinds closed, shine a flashlight beam on the wall.

2. Have your child choose a magnetic letter and hold it in the beam of light so that the shadow of the letter projects against the wall.

3. Then switch roles. Let your child take a turn with the flashlight and try to line the beam of light up with the letter as you hold it up.

To make it easier: *Try using solid shapes, such as circles or squares, which are easier to recognize than letters.*

To make it harder: *Ask your child to call out the letters as their shadows project on the wall. Or encourage pretend play by using your hands to make animal shapes while guessing each other's animals.*

Laundry Basket Push

Use this activity to help your child calm their body when they're over-stimulated, stressed, or otherwise need to regulate. This pushing activity provides heavy work, engaging the muscles and providing movement-related sensory input.

Age: 2+

Prep time: 5 minutes

Activity time: 10 minutes or more

MATERIALS

Plastic rectangular laundry basket or cardboard box

Books, toys, or other safe household items

Clear floor surface

Masking tape (optional)

Cones or other items to weave around (optional)

STEPS

1. Fill a laundry basket with household items. When choosing the items, let your child make a theme or get creative with pretend play ideas. Make sure the basket is heavy enough to provide input to your child's arms but not so heavy that it's difficult to move.

2. Have your child push the basket back and forth across a cleared floor space.

3. Make it fun by timing your child, making a path to follow with masking tape (if using), or inviting them to weave through cones (if using).

To make it easier: *Younger children can push a weighted ball back and forth instead of a laundry basket.*

To make it harder: *Tie a rope to the basket. Your child can alternate between pushing it with their hands and pulling it with the rope while walking backward in a safe space.*

Make Me a Sandwich!

This easy, cozy activity is a common occupational therapy strategy that uses deep pressure to help your child's body calm. Turn it into a fun game by wrapping their body like a sandwich or burrito.

Age: 2+

Prep time: 3 minutes

Activity time: 5 minutes, or more or less time as tolerated

MATERIALS

Blanket or other stretchy material

STEPS

1. Have your child lie on their back with a blanket spread out underneath them.

2. Grab the right side of the blanket and bring it across their chest. Repeat with the left side. Don't cover their neck or face.

3. For added fun, before wrapping up, pretend to add other sandwich ingredients like lettuce, meat, cheese, and ketchup. With each ingredient, use deep arm and leg squeezes to help better prepare your child for the full-body proprioceptive input that comes with being wrapped up.

To make it easier: *If your child seems overwhelmed, let them take control by wrapping their own body.*

To make it harder: *Take your child on a blanket ride by pulling them around on the blanket in an open space. (Consider using a thicker blanket and having your child lie down on their belly or sit up.) Stop, go, spin, pull, and push to give vestibular input as well.*

SKILLS LEARNED	Touch	Smell	Proprioception	Vestibular	Emotional Regulation	Gross Motor Skills
	✋	👃	🙌	⚡	❤️	🤸

Shaving Cream Slide

Slipping and sliding is fun enough by itself, but this activity takes it to another level! It engages most of your child's senses through movement, smell, and texture.

Age: 2+

Prep time: 15 minutes

Activity time: 30 minutes

MATERIALS

Plastic painter tarp or store-bought Slip 'N Slide

Heavy items with safe edges to hold down the tarp

Swimsuits

Multiple cans of plain, unscented shaving cream, or whipped cream for kids under age 2

Toys (optional)

Water from hose or filled kiddie pool

Towels

STEPS

1. Lay the tarp outside on level ground and place the heavy objects on the four corners to hold it down.

2. With both of you wearing swimsuits, spray the cream on the tarp and have your child help spread it around.

3. Get playing! Run, slide, roll, and even bring toys in.

4. Clean up with a hose or a dip in the kiddie pool before drying off with a towel.

To make it easier: *For children under the age of 2, place whipped cream in a kiddie pool or water table. If your child shows tactile aversions, have them use a large paintbrush to spread the cream and encourage exploration based on what they can tolerate.*

To make it harder: *Use other safe textures.*

Breathing Ball

Use this visual breathing technique to help your child settle their breathing and calm their body. Work together, showing that you will make a Hoberman sphere bigger as your child breathes in, then slowly make it smaller as they breathe out. (If you don't have access to a Hoberman sphere, use a balloon.)

Age: 2+
Prep time: 1 minute
Activity time: 15 minutes

MATERIALS

Hoberman sphere or balloon

STEPS

1. Have your child take a deep breath in as you open the Hoberman sphere (or inflate the balloon) so their lungs are filling along with the ball.

2. Close the ball (or deflate the balloon) as you have your child breathe out, modeling the lungs compressing.

3. Repeat 5 to 10 times, at a speed to match their breath rate (about 20 to 40 breaths for children 1 to 6 years of age, with fewer, longer breaths as age increases).

To make it easier: *Instead of using the sphere, help your child practice deep breathing while you simply count. Have them focus on using their nose to inhale and their nose and mouth to exhale. Count at a speed that will help organize their breathing pattern.*

To make it harder: *Have your child open and close the ball on their own, in sync with their breathing. Leave it in an easily accessible space so your child can independently use it to help with self-regulation.*

Bubble Wrap Footprints

Get ready for messy fun while stomping and popping to make colorful footprints. This activity is great for exploring tactile play, managing emotions with changes in sounds, and even controlling the amount of pressure used on the bubble wrap to pop or not pop the bubbles.

Age: 2+

Prep time: 10 minutes

Activity time: 15 minutes

MATERIALS

Old sheet that can get dirty

Large roll of paper or easel paper

Tape

Washable paints

Paper plates or reusable plastic plates

Scissors

Bubble wrap

Wipes or paper towels as needed

STEPS

1. Lay down an old sheet in an open space. Cut and lay down at least 4 to 5 feet of rolled paper on top of the sheet. Tape down the corners of the paper.

2. Add a different color of paint to each plate.

3. Cut two pieces of bubble wrap and wrap them around your child's feet with the bubbles facing outward. Use enough bubble wrap to create two or three layers. Tape the edges together so the bubble wrap stays on your child's feet.

4. Let your child push their bubble-wrapped feet around in a paint color. Then invite them to walk, stomp, jump, or do animal walks across the paper. Use wipes or paper towels to clean up.

To make it easier: *If the texture or sound of the bubble wrap is overwhelming for your child, try plastic wrap instead.*

To make it harder: *Have your kid crawl on their hands and knees, with or without bubble wrap.*

Be the Chef!

This is a great way to introduce your child to various foods. The instructions below use grilled cheese and broccoli, but you can make whatever you and your child want.

Age: 2+
Prep time: 15 minutes
Activity time: 30 minutes

MATERIALS

Ingredients, such as bread and cheese, butter or oil, broccoli, and salt

Recipes for a grilled cheese sandwich and broccoli (written, visual, or spoken)

Cooking items: pan, spatula, microwave-safe dish

Items to serve the food: plates, utensils, napkins

Safe serving containers to pass around the table

STEPS

1. Have your child gather the ingredients and bring them to the work space.

2. Based on the recipe, invite your child to place the cheese slices on the bread, or talk to them about the process, letting them watch from a safe distance as you grill the sandwiches or trim the broccoli.

3. Have your child place the broccoli pieces and a little water into the microwave-safe dish for you to steam. Talk about the look, the smell, and thoughts on how it might taste.

4. Let your child set the table and help you place cooked items on serving plates or in bowls once they're cool enough to touch.

5. Once seated, ask your child to hand or serve items to you. Thank them for all their good work!

Safety tip: *Keep young children away from heat, knives, or other kitchen dangers.*

To make it easier: *Invite your child to be present while you cook—with no pressure to engage.*

To make it harder: *Let your child taste (safe) raw foods and use clean hands to feel their textures.*

Sight and Sound Jars

Make sight and sound jars your child can use to work through big feelings and help calm their body. Sit back and let these sensory experiences help your overwhelmed child, or, if they're ready, use this opportunity to discuss their emotional responses.

Age: 2+
Prep time: 15 minutes
Activity time: 15 minutes

MATERIALS

Dry twigs or small sticks

2 clear disposable water bottles (16 ounces or larger), cleaned and dried, with caps

½ to 1 cup dried rice, beans, or beads

Duct tape and/or hot glue gun with glue sticks

Room-temperature water

Clear glue

Funnel

Glitter

Food coloring (optional)

STEPS

1. To make the sound jar, put the twigs in a bottle, breaking them apart to fit if needed. Add the dried rice, beans, and/or beads. Have an adult glue or duct-tape the cap on.

2. To make the sight jar, fill a bottle three-quarters full with water, then fill it most of the rest of the way with clear glue. Use a funnel to add as much glitter as desired. Add 1 to 2 drops of food coloring (if using). Have an adult glue or duct-tape the cap on.

3. When your child is experiencing big feelings, they can shake the sound jar and listen to the noise, or shake the sight jar and watch the glitter slowly fall.

Safety tip: *If using a hot glue gun, keep it out of reach of your child.*

To make it easier: *Show your child how to take deep breaths while listening to or watching the calming jars.*

To make it harder: *Have your child independently synchronize their breath with the sight jar. Before using the jars, talk about the reasons for your child's big feelings or how the jars help with calming.*

SKILLS
LEARNED

Emotional
Regulation

Oral
Motor Skills

Hearing

Sight

Bubble Mountain

Let your child blow the biggest bubble mountain EVER to help calm their body and transition to harder activities. This is also a great way to work on oral motor strength and stamina.

Age: 2+

Prep time: 5 minutes

Activity time: 10 minutes

MATERIALS

Nontoxic dish soap

Large bowl

Warm water

Spoon

Straws

STEPS

1. Place 2 or 3 small squirts of dish soap into a large bowl, fill it halfway with warm water, and stir with a spoon.

2. Have your child use a straw to blow bubbles in the water, keeping good lip closure around the straw and using big breaths out—trying not to suck water or air back in.

3. Encourage them to get the bubbles as high as possible to make the biggest "bubble mountain"!

To make it easier: *Have your child blow the bubbles as you slowly count to 5. Play songs they like in the background or just provide quiet time, depending on your child's needs.*

To make it harder: *Talk about how the sounds and sights help your child relax and make their body feel calm.*

What's That Smell?

Does your child easily become overstimulated by certain smells? Use this activity to slowly introduce different smells in a fun and relaxing way. Have your child guess the smell of different items without looking!

Age: 2+

Prep time: 10 minutes

Activity time: 15 minutes

MATERIALS

6 mason jars or other sealable containers

6 scented items, such as a cinnamon stick, fruity gummy snack, orange slice, peanut butter, soap, cheesy cracker

Blindfold, such as a sleeping mask or bandanna

STEPS

1. Without your child watching, place a scented item into each jar. Seal the jars and keep them out of sight.

2. Cover your child's eyes with the blindfold and place the jars nearby.

3. Open one jar at a time. Have your child sniff it and guess what kind of item is inside based on the smell.

To make it easier: *Tell your child what items you're using ahead of time, but still have them guess which one is in which container while blindfolded. You could also let them sniff and then provide two or three options to guess from ("Is that cinnamon, orange, or peanut butter?"). If your child doesn't like a certain smell, don't use it.*

To make it harder: *Use items with less distinctive smells, or, if your child approves, try smells they don't prefer (remove the blindfold if needed to prevent overstimulation). Hopefully this will result in both of you laughing at your reactions!*

DIY Outdoor Ninja Course

Get outdoors and use the natural surroundings to challenge your child's balance, body awareness, and comfort with getting their feet off the ground. The materials here are just suggestions—get as creative as you want!

Age: 2+
Prep time: 30 minutes
Activity time: 20 minutes

MATERIALS

4 or 5 stepping-stones or sturdy tree stumps of various heights, if available

12 (1-by-1-foot) wood squares

Rope or pool noodle

1 (4-by-4-inch) board, at least 1 foot long

STEPS

1. Set up an outdoor obstacle course with obstacles a few feet apart. Place the stepping-stones no more than 3 inches apart from each other on a curved line for your child to walk across with alternating feet.

2. Put the wood squares in 2 rows of 6 squares, slightly offset from each other to encourage a zigzag stepping pattern.

3. Place the rope or pool noodle on the ground to jump over and land on two feet.

4. Place the 4-by-4-inch board on the ground to create a "balance beam."

5. Encourage your child to start from the beginning and not to touch the ground, except between obstacles.

6. Repeat as desired. Actively help your child as needed and provide supervision for safety.

To make it easier: *Hold your child's hand to help them balance.*

To make it harder: *Encourage hopping on one or two feet on different stepping-stones or walking sideways or backward on the balance beam.*

Visual
Spatial Skills

Memory

Planning and
Problem-Solving

Tactile Sensory Bin

Get your child ready to engage in pretend play using different dry, wet, or sticky textures. This activity is great for your child to search, explore, and tolerate various textures. It is also a helpful sensory tool for calming the body.

Age: 3+
Prep time: 15 minutes
Activity time: 30 minutes

MATERIALS

Large mat or blanket that can get dirty

Large, shallow storage container

6 cups (more or less, depending on container size) of a tactile substance, such as sand, dried rice, dried beans, shaving cream, etc.

Sandbox toys: small shovels, buckets, funnels, etc.

Other toys: animal figures, cars, etc.

STEPS

1. Spread the mat on a tabletop or floor and put the storage container on top of it. Fill the container halfway with the sand or other substance and the toys.

2. Let your child freely explore and engage in pretend play.

3. As your child will tolerate it, hide items under the surface of the substance and have your child find them by feeling around.

To make it easier: *Let your child touch the substance without their hands, such as by pushing a stick or shovel around in it.*

To make it harder: *Let your child put their feet in the bin or mix two or more textures. Increase cognitive, visual, and sensory processing skills by hiding puzzle pieces in a dry substance and having your child find them and complete the puzzle.*

Guess That Shape

Does your child have a hard time identifying objects or textures without looking at them? This is a great activity to build on recognizing objects just by touch. Let's practice guessing shapes without looking!

Age: 3+
Prep time: 20 minutes
Activity time: 15 minutes

MATERIALS

Scissors or utility knife

Shoebox or old cardboard box

Shapes from shape sorter or different foam building block shapes

Crayons, markers, or colored pencils

Blank index cards

Timer (optional)

STEPS

1. Cut a 5-inch-diameter hole either at the top or bottom middle portion of the box, adjusting the size as needed.

2. Place 2 or 3 of each shape into the box, such as circular, triangular, and square shapes.

3. Draw a circle, triangle, and square, or other matching shapes, on each index card.

4. Hand your child a card and invite them to feel around without peeking to find the shape shown on the card.

Safety tip: *Keep the scissors or knife out of reach of your child.*

To make it easier: *Allow for trial and error, and let your child peek if needed.*

To make it harder: *Work on fine motor skills by having your child draw the shapes on the index cards, or add other new shapes to find. Or turn it into an exciting game by setting a time limit!*

Airplane Catch

Strengthen your child's belly muscles and get deep pressure to their arms as they push a ball back and forth while holding an airplane position on their belly.

Age: 3+
Prep time: 1 minute
Activity time: 10 minutes

MATERIALS

Kickball or soccer ball

STEPS

1. Lie on the floor with your child, on your bellies, facing head to head, 3 to 4 feet apart from each other.

2. Raise your arms and legs off the ground to imitate an airplane position. Have your child hold the position as long as possible as you push the ball back and forth between you, resting as needed.

To make it easier: *Add visual support by putting masking tape on the ground to mark the space your child should stay within. Hold the airplane position for no more than 5 seconds.*

To make it harder: *See how long your child can hold the airplane position while pushing the ball back and forth. Change the game using different positions, such as doing a crab walk or trying to kick the ball into a goal.*

Popcorn Pop!

This is a fantastic way to provide deep pressure and help calm your child's body. Use a body sock or other stretchy material to provide deep pressure and turn it into a fun popcorn game by inviting your child to push out on the body sock as hard as they can.

Age: 3+
Prep time: 5 minutes
Activity time: 5 to 10 minutes

MATERIALS

Sensory body sock or stretchy sheet or blanket

STEPS

1. Place the body sock, stretchy sheet, or blanket around your child's body—without covering their head—or have them wrap themselves up while lying on their back.

2. Have your child curl their arms and legs into a ball.

3. Do a countdown and then have your child quickly extend their arms and legs, like popping popcorn shooting out against the blanket material.

4. Repeat as many times as desired.

To make it easier: *Do the popping motion without the body sock first, or only do it for a few seconds.*

To make it harder: *Add music, and when the music stops, have your child "pop"!*

SKILLS
LEARNED

Proprioception

Gross Motor
Skills

Attention

Planning and
Problem-Solving

Moon Walk

Put on your astronaut suits! It's time to collect some moon rocks while walking across the moon. This obstacle course is a fun way to work on body awareness, balance, and responding to different sensory inputs when navigating across and over various surfaces.

Age: 3+

Prep time: 15 minutes

Activity time: 15 minutes

MATERIALS

Masking tape

2 or 3 tennis balls or other small balls

Chair tall enough to crawl under

Step-up object(s), such as a step stool or stepping-stones

Large pillows

Blanket

Laundry basket

Larger objects, such as large balls or stuffed animals (optional)

STEPS

1. Use masking tape to mark the start of the obstacle course. Scatter the "moon rocks" (tennis balls) throughout the course.

2. Place the chair a few feet away and the step-up object(s) a few feet away from the chair.

3. Place the pillows a few feet farther away and cover them with the blanket.

4. Mark the end of the obstacle course with masking tape and set the laundry basket there.

5. Have your child pick up the moon rocks as they crawl under the chair, step over or across the step-up(s), and then walk on the "moon's surface" (the pillows with the blanket over it), finally placing the moon rocks in the laundry basket.

6. Praise them for their success and repeat as desired.

To make it easier: *Provide assistance as needed, such as holding your child's hand, breaking down the course into single steps, and/or demonstrating what to do.*

To make it harder: *Bring the moon rocks back to the "spaceship" (whatever designated area you choose). Use masking tape to mark the ground with a curvy line and have your child push the laundry basket along this trail to the spaceship. For increased heavy work, add other objects, such as large balls or stuffed animals, to retrieve while completing the obstacle course.*

Cardboard Car Speedway

Let your child decorate their own cardboard car and ride it down a hill! Use this activity to engage your child's vestibular system through the use of quick movements.

Age: 3+

Prep time: 15 minutes

Activity time: 20 minutes

MATERIALS

Large, sturdy cardboard box (large enough to hold your child)

Packing tape

Drawing utensils (optional)

Very large piece of cardboard or several pieces taped together, to use as a slide

STEPS

1. Remove the top portion of the box or tape it open so your child can go inside and hold on to the flap. Decorate the box if desired.

2. Place a large piece of cardboard at the top of a slight incline as a slide for the cardboard box. Use the packing tape as needed to repair any rips.

3. Have your child place the box at the top of the cardboard slide, sit inside it, and shift their weight/scoot their bottom to get started going down the hill.

4. To help prevent your child from getting over-stimulated, add proprioceptive activities such as deep squeezes in between trips, or have them get some fun heavy work by using animal walks to get the box back up the hill.

To make it easier: *Hold on to your child as they go down the hill in the box or just let them sit on their bottom (not in a box) and slide down.*

To make it harder: *Add more vestibular input by having your child roll down the hill like a log (not in a box), as long as the space is safe and clear.*

Reverse Crunch on a Ball

Help your child work on tolerating different head positions while maintaining their balance. In this game, they'll lean back to retrieve toys and throw them at a target!

Age: 3+
Prep time: 5 minutes
Activity time: 15 minutes

MATERIALS

Exercise ball

Different colored beanbags or small stuffed animals

Bucket or another item to use as a target

Step stool (optional)

STEPS

1. Place the exercise ball in the middle of an open space. Place the beanbags or stuffed animals behind the ball, with the bucket or other target in front of it.

2. Help your child onto the exercise ball with their back facing the items, either by lifting your child or providing a step stool. Hold their hips for support.

3. Invite your child to lean or lie back to reach for an item. Don't let go of their hips and support the ball or your child as needed.

4. Encourage your child to sit up without using their hands for support, crossing their arms if needed.

5. Once sitting, cheer them on as they throw the item into the target. Repeat until all the items are collected or thrown.

6. Provide proprioceptive input as needed, such as bouncing the ball on breaks, or offering deep pressure or heavy work activities.

To make it easier: *If your child shows fear at leaning their head backward while on the ball, do this game lying on the floor instead of on a ball. Hold their ankles for support if needed.*

To make it harder: *Work on memory skills by calling out 2 or 3 items for your child to gather in a specific order.*

Sensory Strategy Cards

Create sensory strategy cards with different activities to help your child wake up or calm down different parts of their body. These cards are great to keep on hand and use whenever your child is having a large sensory response. They can be kept in a Sensory Calming Bin (page 30) or taken on the road wherever you go. You can also talk with your child's school team about incorporating these cards at school.

Age: 3+

Prep time: 30 minutes

Activity time: 15 minutes or as needed

MATERIALS

1 or 2 sheets (8½-by-11-inch) paper

Pencil or pen

Markers or crayons (optional)

Laminator (optional)

Scissors

Small storage box or Velcro to attach cards to a large piece of paper

STEPS

1. Fold a sheet of paper in half 4 times to make 16 squares.

2. Draw a line in each of the creases to define each square.

3. Create 1 to 3 strategies for each sensory system you want to work on. Write one strategy in each square (card) and, if possible, draw an associated picture. Examples:

   - **Auditory:** Listen to a favorite song. Wear noise-canceling headphones.

   - **Oral processing:** Chew gum or a crunchy snack.

   - **Proprioception:** Squish into pillows. Roll up in a blanket. Ask for deep squeezes.

   - **Tactile:** Use a sensory bin, squishy ball, soft stuffed animal, or blanket.

   - **Vestibular:** Swing, spin, hang upside-down.

   - **Visual:** Turn off the lights. Color in a coloring book.

4. Laminate the paper if desired and cut out each card.

5. Store the cards in a box or use Velcro on the backs of the cards to stick them to a large piece of paper for storage. Keep them handy to use as needed.

6. Let your child choose activities to help regulate their body, or offer them card choices when they experience big feelings.

Ball Fishing

Like Reverse Crunch on a Ball (page 51), this activity helps your child work on tolerating different head positions while also strengthening their belly muscles—all during a fun fishing game. Have your child really work on keeping their balance so they don't fall into the "water"!

Age: 4+

Prep time: 5 minutes

Activity time: 10 minutes

MATERIALS

Exercise ball

Fish toys or other toys

Bucket

Step stool (optional)

STEPS

1. Place an exercise ball in the middle of an open space and spread the toys out on the floor, some within arm's reach from the ball and some out of arm's reach.

2. Place the bucket 1 to 2 feet away from the ball, just enough distance to throw. For a challenge, place the bucket farther away or off to the side..

3. Lifting your child or using a step stool if necessary, help your child lie on their belly on the ball. Hold their ankles for support.

4. Encourage your child to walk forward on their hands with their legs staying on the ball to "fish" (reach) for the items and place them in the "catch" bucket.

5. Praise your child for collecting all the fish!

To make it easier: *If your child shows fear when their head is facing downward while on the ball, get rid of the ball and have them lie on their belly on the floor or on a scooter, pulling themselves forward with only their hands to reach for the items.*

To make it harder: *Work on memory skills by calling out 2 or 3 items for your child to gather in a specific order.*

Map My Feelings

Let your child explore all their body's messages about feelings by creating a life-size self-portrait to draw their emotions on. They'll increase awareness of their underlying body messages and where they might feel these in their body to help them link those messages to different emotional experiences.

Age: 4+
Prep time: 10 minutes
Activity time: 30 minutes

MATERIALS

Easel paper or rolled brown paper

Crayons or markers

STEPS

1. On the floor, roll out enough paper for your child to lie down on.

2. Have your child lie on their back on the paper. Trace their outline with a crayon.

3. Ask basic questions related to feelings and help them figure out where these feelings happen in their body and how their body responds. Start with guiding questions, but add support as needed. Give examples of feelings and even talk about how your own body reacts—this will help get your child thinking. Suggestions include:

   - "When you're happy, how does your body feel?" Possible answers: I want to smile; my heart feels warm; I have good feelings.

   - "When you're angry, how does your body feel?" Possible answers: My heart beats fast; my chest feels tight; my hands clench; my eyebrows furrow.

   - "When you're nervous, how does your body feel?" Possible answers: I have butterflies in my stomach; my hands get sweaty; I have a hard time turning on my voice.

4. Help your child picture how their emotions feel in their body by inviting them to draw on the outlined body shape. For example, you might suggest they draw butterflies in their stomach to show how they feel when they're nervous.

To make it easier: *Provide your child with ideas and choices related to emotions and associated body reactions.*

To make it harder: *Really let your child problem-solve and explore all these emotions and body messages to independently identify what they're feeling and how it shows up in their body.*

Body-Level Messages

We all have needs, and when our body needs something, it sends us a message. For example, when we're tired, we yawn and our eyelids feel heavy. Help your child get in touch with their body's messages by creating pictures or stories that show how their body feels and responds to different body needs.

Age: 4+

Prep time: 10 minutes

Activity time: 30 minutes

MATERIALS

Multiple sheets of paper

Drawing and writing utensils or printed images from online or a magazine

Glue sticks

STEPS

1. On each sheet of paper write, "I know I'm _____ when _____." Each sheet should focus on a physical need your child may need to work on, such as hunger, thirst, bathroom needs, body temperature (hot/cold), tiredness, pain, and so on.

2. For each physical need, have your child think of 1 to 3 body-level messages to fill in the blanks. For example: "I know I'm thirsty when my throat feels dry" or "I know I'm cold when I get goose bumps."

3. Leave space underneath the sentence and invite your child to draw or glue pictures that match the feelings in the space.

To make it easier: *Provide choices of body-level messages.*

To make it harder: *Discuss feelings in the moment and have your child focus on what their body is feeling and how their body is responding.*

Chapter Three

Motor Skills

"MOTOR SKILLS" IS A TECHNICAL TERM for using your muscles. *Gross motor skills* involve large muscles and whole-body movements needed for balance, coordination, body awareness, strength, and endurance. We use them for activities such as sitting, standing, walking, and running. *Fine motor skills* involve smaller muscles, particularly in the hand, and include hand-eye coordination, hand and finger strength, and using two hands together—necessary skills for writing, drawing, and more. *Oral motor skills* use the muscles in and around the mouth and are vital for eating and speaking. Children with cerebral palsy, Down syndrome, or other physical disabilities and developmental delays can benefit from the activities in this chapter, as can children with autism spectrum disorder, sensory processing disorder, and ADHD. But any child will enjoy these games as a fun and functional way to build motor skills!

Lick Your Lips

Does your child tend to put too much food in their mouth at one time, or have trouble moving food around with their tongue? Try this fun game of placing food on the corners of their mouth to practice moving their tongue side to side.

Age: 1+
Prep time: 10 minutes
Activity time: 15 minutes

MATERIALS

Gooey food, such as applesauce, yogurt, or pudding

STEPS

1. Place the food on both corners of your child's mouth where their lips meet, or invite your child to do it.

2. Encourage your child to move their tongue to each side to get as much of the food as possible.

3. If your child doesn't have any food aversions, make it into a fun game. Tell them not to look and let them guess the food as they lick it off.

4. If your child tends to overstuff their mouth or eat too quickly, make it into a fun game of taking small bites and eating slowly.

Safety tip: If your child has significant feeding needs, consult with your occupational therapist or other medical provider before doing this activity.

To make it easier: *Use a mirror so your child can look for the food and see how they can move their tongue side to side.*

To make it harder: *Without food, see how fast your child can move their tongue side to side, touching the inside of their cheeks while keeping their tongue in their mouth.*

Dump Truck Races

Who doesn't love a good race? Help your child work on coordination, balance, and strength by using their hands and knees to push their dump truck as they race to the finish line.

Age: 1+

Prep time: 10 minutes

Activity time: 20 minutes

MATERIALS

String or masking tape

Soft surface, such as grass or foam mats

Items to fill up the trucks: small rocks, toys, etc.

Bucket

2 dump trucks or other outdoor push toys

Timer (optional)

STEPS

1. Use two pieces of string or masking tape to mark the start and finish lines on the soft surface, about 6 to 8 feet apart.

2. Place the rocks or other small items at the starting line and the bucket at the finish line.

3. Have your child grab a dump truck and get on their knees at the starting line. Take another truck and race them, or simply time their efforts with a timer (if using).

4. When you say "Go," have your child place as many rocks as they want in the truck bed, then stay on their hands and knees as they push the truck to the finish line.

5. Have them dump the rocks into the bucket to complete the activity.

To make it easier: *Have your child stay seated or standing, whichever they prefer, and push the truck on a table, using only as many rocks as needed to get just the right amount of heavy work.*

To make it harder: *Have your child use different positions while pushing the dump truck, such as pushing the truck with a foot or crab walking while pushing the truck. Boost the sensory demand by having them push the truck across sand, mud, or even shaving cream!*

Reach for the Stars

Build a simple obstacle course using play and household items to encourage your child to explore different positions and reach with their hands. This obstacle course is specifically designed to help younger children or children with motor challenges develop these skills in a safe environment.

Age: 1+
Prep time: 15 minutes
Activity time: 15 minutes

MATERIALS

Foam or gym mats

Pop-up tunnel or a sheet to create a tunnel

Soft items to crawl up and over: pillows, foam wedges, soft cubes, beanbag chair

Activity mat with hanging toys (for kids 2 and under)

A line to hang up simple items: toy links, mobile animals, or cardboard shapes (for kids 3 and older)

Clothespins, tape, or ribbons to hang items on the line

STEPS

1. Place the mats on the floor in an open space.

2. Open the pop-up tunnel or create your own by placing a sheet over sturdy stools or chairs, or between couches.

3. Using the soft items, create a small incline for your child to crawl up and over.

4. Complete the obstacle course by placing the mat or hanging items within arm's reach, according to the following age guidelines:

   - **2 years:** Use an activity mat and encourage your child to crawl under and reach up to hit the hanging items.

   - **3 to 5 years:** Encourage your child to get up tall on both knees to reach for the items and pull them off, if possible.

   - **5 to 6 years:** Let them try half kneeling or balancing on one leg while standing to reach for the items, and encourage fine motor skills by having them untie the items from the line.

Pass the Juice

This so-grown-up activity will help your child work on their pouring skills to encourage the fine motor skill of using two hands together. Turn it into a game and see who can pour the most in 1 minute!

Age: 1+

Prep time: 10 to 15 minutes

Activity time: 20 minutes

MATERIALS

2 or more sturdy plastic cups or jars

Substance to fill the containers: water, sand, dried beans, beads, etc.

2 or more empty milk jugs or juice jugs

Timer

STEPS

1. Have your child fill a plastic cup with water or another substance, offering help as needed. Have them pick up the other plastic cup and pour the substance from one cup into the other. Continue to pour back and forth, encouraging them not to spill.

2. Repeat step 1, using milk jugs instead of cups.

3. Time your child and have them go as quickly as they can without spilling. How many times can they pour back and forth in 1 minute?

To make it easier: *Work on pouring or dumping a liquid or dry item from a cup into a large open container.*

To make it harder: *Add gross motor challenges while pouring, such as kneeling, squatting, or even balancing on a balance board!*

Pipe Cleaners and Pom-Poms

Have your child work on developing their pincer grasp, manipulation skills, and hand-eye coordination by picking up colorful pom-poms and pipe cleaners and filling a bottle to the top!

Age: 1+

Prep time: 15 minutes

Activity time: 15 minutes

MATERIALS

About 12 pipe cleaners

15 or more colored pom-poms (different sizes and textures, if possible)

2 or more clean, empty water bottles

Cardboard cereal box (optional)

Utility knife (optional)

STEPS

1. On a table or on the floor, lay out the pipe cleaners, pom-poms, and water bottles.

2. Let your child explore at first. Sit back, observe, and enjoy how they interact with the different items.

3. Have your child insert the pipe cleaners and pom-poms into the bottle opening. You can either show them or tell them how.

4. For more challenging fun (if desired), cut various angled slots in a cardboard cereal box with the utility knife. Have your child work on inserting the pipe cleaners and pom-poms into these slots.

Safety tip: *Keep the utility knife out of your child's reach. Also, be careful of small objects with young children.*

To make it easier: *Help your child with manipulating items as needed, and use a wide-mouth bottle.*

To make it harder: *Have your child string small beads onto the pipe cleaners before inserting them into the bottle. They can also use kitchen tongs to pick up the pom-poms and place them into the container.*

We Got the Beat

Make some music using pots, pans, or any household items you can think of! Follow the beat and dance along to help your child work on imitation skills, hand use, and coordination.

Age: 1+
Prep time: 10 minutes
Activity time: 30 minutes

MATERIALS

"Drumsticks": sticks, wooden spoons, real drumsticks

"Drums": pots, pans, buckets, real drums

STEPS

1. Start simple: Bang two hands or drumsticks on the drum 2 to 4 times and have your child repeat after you. Increase the number of repetitions for your child to imitate.

2. Try changing the rhythm, alternating hands or drumsticks while drumming, and banging in this pattern 2 to 4 times, then have your child do the same. Get creative.

3. Encourage your child to dance along with your drumming. Have them do different moves, like clapping one or both hands on their legs to the beat. Join them!

To make it easier: *Keep it simple, using two hands at once and slowly increasing the number of beats.*

To make it harder: *Have your child do tricky dance moves, like touching their left hand to their right leg and their right hand to their left leg.*

Straw Race

Get out your straws and get ready to blow, as you and your child crawl on your bellies in a challenging race to the finish line! This activity helps develop oral motor skills by strengthening your child's lip use and building up their breathing endurance.

Age: 2+

Prep time: 5 minutes

Activity time: 15 minutes

MATERIALS

Masking tape

2 or more disposable or soft reusable straws

Cotton balls or pom-poms

STEPS

1. In an open space, use the masking tape to mark start and finish lines on the floor 3 or 4 feet apart.

2. Have each racer take a straw and a cotton ball. Get down on the floor on your bellies at the start line.

3. Keeping your lips closed around the straw, show your child how to blow out with a long blow to push the cotton ball forward.

4. Army-crawl forward to keep up with the ball, blowing it toward the finish line. See who can get there first!

To make it easier: *Have your child sit at a table with their feet on the ground and good support from a chair back. They can practice blowing through the straw to make the cotton ball move. Encourage your child to sit as tall as possible for big breaths and help them close their lips around the straw as needed.*

To make it harder: *Increase the length of the race. Encourage other forms of movement instead of an army crawl, like using a bear walk or a floor scooter while blowing the ball to the finish line.*

Straws and Snowballs

You *can* play with "snowballs" even in the summer! Like Straw Race (page 69), this activity focuses on the oral motor skills of closing your lips, but it also helps kids build strength for blowing out and sucking in.

Age: 2+

Prep time: 5 minutes

Activity time: 15 minutes

MATERIALS

About 15 cotton balls

1 or more drinking straws

Small dish or container

Timer (optional)

STEPS

1. Place the "snowballs" (cotton balls) and straw on a cleared table with the dish to the left or right.

2. Have your child sit down at the table, with good back support and both feet on the floor or a footrest.

3. Have your child take the straw, close their lips around it, and practice sucking air in for a few seconds.

4. Have your child hold the straw with one hand, place the straw onto a snowball, and suck in so it "attaches" to the straw. Use another straw to demonstrate if needed.

5. By holding their breath for a few seconds, the child can then move the straw over the dish and blow out to "throw" the snowball into the container.

6. Repeat until all the snowballs are cleaned up.

To make it easier: *Have your child practice just holding the snowball on the straw for a few seconds with a big breath in.*

To make it harder: *Have a friend or sibling join. Who can clean up their snowballs the fastest? Time your child to see if they can beat their previous score.*

Feed the Dragon

The dragon is hungry and all the animals need your child's help getting him some food as fast as they can—but don't wake him up while he's sleeping! This activity helps build motor skills such as balance, coordination, endurance, and manipulation of objects.

Age: 2+

Prep time: 15 minutes

Activity time: 20 minutes

MATERIALS

Index cards

Marker

Pretend play food

Large serving spoons or tongs (optional)

Medium container

Stuffed dragon or other "ferocious" animal, or a picture of a dragon

STEPS

1. Use the index cards and marker to create "movement cards." On each card, write and/or draw an age-appropriate movement like jumping, crawling, hopping on one foot, or skipping.

2. Put the pretend food and serving spoons or tongs in the container and place them next to the cards on one side of a room. Put the sleeping dragon on the other side of the room.

3. Have your child pick a movement card and use the movement on that card (hop, crawl, etc.) to carry a piece of pretend play food on a serving spoon, or in tongs or their hands, across the room to feed the dragon. Don't drop your food, or you might wake the dragon!

To make it easier: *Have your child get a piece of food and walk over to feed the dragon without any special movements.*

To make it harder: *In an open area, blindfold your child and give them directions on how to get to the dragon to feed him the food. Stay close so they don't bump into things.*

Penny-Eating Monster

Turn a tennis ball into a penny-eating monster! Your child will feed it coins while working on finger and hand skills.

Age: 2+
Prep time: 15 minutes
Activity time: 15 minutes

MATERIALS

Utility knife

Tennis ball

Glue

Decorations: googly eyes, feathers, etc. (optional)

Coins

STEPS

1. Use the utility knife to cut a 3-inch slit across one of the gray lines on the tennis ball. Open and close the hole to help stretch it out. This is the monster's mouth.

2. If your child is interested, they can decorate the ball with googly eyes, etc.

3. Spread some coins on the floor or a table. Have your child pick up one coin at a time to feed the monster. The goal is for your child to hold the tennis ball with one hand and place the coin in the "mouth" with the other hand. Observe how your child picks up the coins.

   - For children under 3, they may use all their fingers to try to scrape up the coin.

   - For older children, work on having them use their thumb and pointer finger (and maybe middle finger) to pick up the coin using a pincer grasp.

4. How many coins can your child get into the monster's mouth in 1 minute?

Safety tip: *Keep the utility knife out of your child's reach.*

To make it easier: *Have your child practice transferring the coins between their hands. Use pom-poms or other items if the coins are too hard to grasp, or if your child tends to put objects in their mouth.*

To make it harder: *Replace the coins with pom-poms and use kitchen tongs, chopsticks, or alligator clips to pick up the pom-poms and feed the monster.*

Hold a Pose!

How long can your child hold yoga poses and other body positions without falling down? This is a great way to work on balance, strength, and coordination, while also learning a few fun and easy yoga poses.

Age: 2+

Prep time: 5 minutes

Activity time: 20 minutes

MATERIALS

Stack of yoga cards or pictures of different yoga poses found online

Soft surface, such as a yoga mat or gym mat

Timer

STEPS

1. Show your child a picture of the yoga position, or, if your child already knows the name of the position, call out the name. Age-appropriate ideas include:

   - **2 to 3 years:** Cat pose, bridge pose, child pose
   - **3 to 5 years:** Boat pose, cobra pose, downward dog pose
   - **5 to 6 years:** Tree pose, eagle pose, warrior pose

2. Have your child hold the pose as long as possible without falling down.

3. Try a variety of poses and have other kids join for added fun.

To make it easier: *Help your child hold the position for just 5 seconds, working toward longer times.*

To make it harder: *Have your child close their eyes to challenge their balance even more.*

DIY Balance Board

Make an easy homemade balance board to help your child work on gross motor and sensory processing skills. You can also add it to any of the obstacle courses or other activities in this book to help work on balance. Buy the materials precut at a hardware store, or cut them yourself.

Age: 2+

Prep time: 30 minutes

Activity time: As long as needed

MATERIALS

Sandpaper

1 (2-foot-long) piece of wood (ideally ¾ inch thick and 10 inches wide)

Patterned or colored duct tape or paint (optional)

1 (2-foot-long) PVC pipe (aim for 1½-inch diameter)

STEPS

1. Sand the wood if needed to avoid splinters.

2. If your child is interested, help them decorate the wood with the duct tape or paint.

3. Place the PVC pipe on a carpeted or grassy surface and put the wood plank over it.

4. Have your child get on the board and see how long they can keep their balance, holding their hands if needed.

Safety tip: *Don't place the balance board on a hard or smooth surface where it can easily slide.*

To make it easier: *Have your child try to balance on their knees. (Kneepads or cushions might be needed.)*

To make it harder: *Engage in a game of catch while on the balance board.*

Hanging the Laundry

Pee-yew, those are some dirty clothes there! Have your child "wash," wring out, and hang clothes on a homemade clothesline—a fun way to work on fine motor skills such as hand strength, object manipulation, and using two hands.

Age: 3+
Prep time: 15 minutes
Activity time: 20 minutes

MATERIALS

String, 1 to 2 feet long

2 chairs or other objects to hang the string on

About 10 clothespins

Towels, if inside

Bucket of warm water

Soap (optional)

5 or so small items of clothing: doll clothes, outgrown infant clothes, etc.

STEPS

1. Set up a homemade clothesline, tying the string between the two chairs at your child's eye level. Attach the clothespins to the line and place the towels underneath (if indoors).

2. Fill the bucket with water and soap (if using) and stir to create bubbles. Place the clothes near one chair.

3. Ask your child to reach overhead while sitting or kneeling and collect all the clothespins. Encourage them to use a pincer grasp to take the clothespins off the line and set them next to the clothes.

4. Now ask your child to take an item of clothing and use both hands to dunk it into the bucket. Have them pull the item out and show them how to use both hands rotating in opposite directions to wring out the water over the bucket.

5. Finally, have them grab 1 or 2 clothespins and reach overhead to hang the clothes on the line, pinching the top of the clothespin with one hand to open it while the other hand positions the clothing item.

6. Invite your child to wash and hang each piece of clothing.

Dress-Up Relay Race

Who would your child like to "be" today? Let your child pick a dress-up theme, then stand on one leg, hop, skip, and get on their clothes as fast as they can to work on balance and coordination.

Age: 3+

Prep time: 15 minutes

Activity time: 15 minutes

MATERIALS

5 pieces of dress-up clothes: shirt, pants, socks, hat or crown, gloves

5 storage bins

Timer

STEPS

1. Place each clothing item in a different bin.

2. Spread out the bins in a line, curve, circle, or other pattern.

3. Start the timer and have your child perform a new movement every time they go to a bin to put on a new item of clothing. For example: Hop on two legs to get a shirt and put it on; slither like a snake to the pants; stand on one leg at a time to put them on; and so on.

4. Once they've visited all the bins, stop the timer! How fast did your child go? Can they go faster next time?

To make it easier: *Scrunch up the clothing with the openings showing to help your child get their body parts in. Let them sit down as needed, and don't use the timer.*

To make it harder: *Use clothing with zippers, snaps, or buttons.*

Paper Plate Skates

Help your child work on balance and coordination by giving them paper plates to "skate" across the floor on. Be careful—this one's fun, but it can be tricky!

Age: 3+
Prep time: 5 minutes
Activity time: 15 minutes

MATERIALS

2 paper plates

STEPS

1. Set up two paper plates on a smooth surface, such as a hardwood or linoleum floor.

2. Have your child take off their socks and put each foot on a separate paper plate. They can now glide and slide across the floor, pushing forward one leg at a time while keeping each foot on its plate.

To make it easier: *Let your child keep their socks on and use masking tape to fasten the plates to their feet.*

To make it harder: *Set up cones or other objects to weave around. Add a ball and play catch while skating to further challenge your child's balance, hand-eye coordination, and attention skills.*

Dough Letters

Help your child build hand strength and work on letter formation with a game of Dough Letters. Once they remove all the beads from the play dough, they can use the dough to form letters.

Age: 3+

Prep time: 20 minutes

Activity time: 30 minutes

MATERIALS

10 or more pieces of construction paper

Black marker

2 or 3 different colors of play dough (see page 166 to make your own)

Beads, buttons, and/or glass pebbles

STEPS

1. On each piece of construction paper, use the marker to write a capital letter. Use as many letters and pieces of paper as you want.

2. Flatten a sheet of one color of play dough on a table, stick beads in it, then roll it into a ball so it's full of beads.

3. Present the letters and the beaded play dough to your child. Their task is to get rid of all the beads so they can use the play dough to trace the letters you've made.

4. Invite your child to search for and remove the beads using a pincer grasp.

5. Show them how to roll out the play dough like a snake to help create lines. Invite your child to use the dough lines to trace a letter on the construction paper.

6. Repeat for each new letter, using new colors of play dough, as desired.

To make it easier: *Instead of letters, draw shapes, curves, and/or angled lines.*

To make it harder: *Let your child be the one to put the beads into the play dough.*

Dough Art

Drawing, cutting shapes, and practicing writing letters is more fun in play dough! This activity helps children learn the right amount of strength and pressure needed while holding a writing utensil, and it's a great way to warm up the body for handwriting tasks.

Age: 3+
Prep time: 10 minutes
Activity time: 30 minutes

MATERIALS

3 or 4 colors of play dough (see page 166 to make your own)

Roller

Items to "write" in the play dough: cotton swabs, toothpicks, or old pencils

Child scissors

STEPS

1. Roll out 2 colors of play dough with the roller and have your child stand up and push it down flat by pressing down hard with extended arms and flat palms.

2. Let your child use an item to draw shapes in the dough. For children over 4, observe the type of grasp they're using and, if possible, encourage them to use 3 or 4 fingers ("tripod" or "quadrupod" grasp) to write with.

   * **3 to 4 years:** Draw a circle and then a cross in your play dough and invite your child to do the same.

   * **4 to 5 years:** Have them copy or independently draw squares, triangles, and diagonal lines.

   * **5 to 6 years:** Have them draw upper- and lowercase letters, either from memory or by copying.

3. Have your child cut out different shapes from the play dough. Encourage them to use a thumb-up position while cutting and to use the non-cutting hand to help rotate the dough and cut out the shapes more smoothly.

To make it easier: *Lightly draw shapes in the play dough and have your child trace over or deepen them. They can even use their pointer finger instead of a cotton swab to draw.*

To make it harder: *Roll out long cylindrical snake shapes with the dough and let your child form letters with them.*

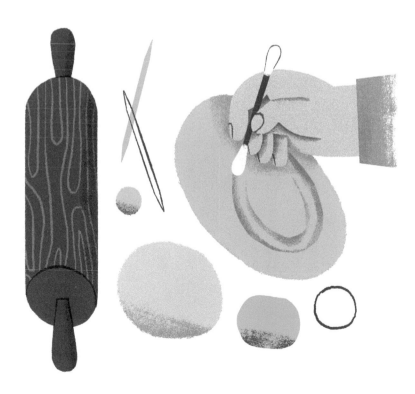

SKILLS
LEARNED

Fine Motor
Skills

Visual
Spatial Skills

Hand-Eye
Coordination

Pin the Tail on the Bunny

Your child will cut out different shapes and glue them together to pin the tail—and the ears, and the legs—on the bunny. Drawing, cutting, and assembling shapes are all great ways to work on fine motor and visual skills.

Age: 3+

Prep time: 10 minutes

Activity time: 15 minutes

MATERIALS

2 sheets of paper

Colored pencils, markers, or crayons

Child scissors

Glue sticks

STEPS

1. On a piece of paper, draw the following items for your child, spread out over the paper: medium circle with a bunny face, 2 bunny ears (triangular like), a tail (small circle), a body (large oval), and 4 legs (rectangles).

2. Place another piece of paper on the table as the "background."

3. Have your child cut out the shapes, using a thumb-up hand grip, staying as close as possible to the lines while cutting, and using their other "helper" hand to rotate the paper as needed.

4. Have your child glue body parts on the "background" paper.

5. As your child works, step back and observe. Are they gluing the body parts in the right places? If not, ask guiding questions like these:

   - "How does the bunny look to you?"
   - "Are the body parts facing the right way?"
   - "What is different about this piece?"
   - "Do you want to turn this one to face the other way?"

   Also provide visual support, such as drawing a line on the bottom of the page to represent the grass to help your child correctly place the bunny pieces.

6. The goal is for them to place the pieces in the right location, but cheer them on for their efforts!

To make it easier: *Cut the pieces for them. Place or glue 1 or 2 pieces to help your child understand the direction of item placement.*

To make it harder: *Have your child draw the shapes for the bunny. Get creative and use different animals. Can your child cut an elephant trunk? Or a shark fin?*

Safari Walk

For this adventure, you'll work with your child to create an obstacle course with household items to navigate using kangaroo hops, ostrich jumps, and other animal walks. It's more than just fun—it's also a great activity for developing gross and fine motor skills in addition to working on memory and the ability to follow directions.

Age: 3+

Prep time: 20 minutes

Activity time: 15 minutes (based on 4 or 5 repetitions)

MATERIALS

Crayons or markers

4 pieces (8-by-10-inch) card stock paper

Child scissors

Rope, pool noodle, masking tape, or stick to use as a "jumping log"

STEPS

1. Have your child draw and cut out 4 or more large circles from the card stock to create different watering holes. Focus on your child using a thumb-up scissor grip and using their helper hand to rotate the paper.

2. Set up the obstacle course: Place the watering holes 6 inches apart. Set up the "jumping log" by placing the rope, pool noodle, or stick on the ground to jump over, or, if needed, placing a strip of masking tape on the floor instead.

3. **Watering holes:** Invite your child to hop and land on two feet on each watering hole like a kangaroo.

4. **Log jump:** Have your child jump as high as they can over the jumping log and land with two feet together, like an ostrich.

5. **Animal walks:** Challenge your child to prowl like a lion, slither like a snake, gallop like a zebra, stomp like an elephant, etc. Demonstrate the different "walks" if needed.

6. Now repeat! Can your child remember all the steps? Give cues as needed.

To make it easier: *Thicken the circle lines if needed to help your child with cutting accuracy or cut out the shapes for them.*

To make it harder: *Encourage hopping on one foot across the watering holes. Set the log jump higher off the ground.*

Paint Here or There

This activity gets messy, but it's a ton of fun. Your child will get into different positions to work on strength, balance, and sensory processing skills while painting with their hands—and feet!

Age: 4+
Prep time: 10 minutes
Activity time: 20 minutes

MATERIALS

Painter's blanket or old blanket

Masking tape

Rolled paper, 2 feet of length per activity

Paper plates

Washable paints

Wet and dry rags

Exercise ball

Smock or old clothes

STEPS

1. Place the painter's blanket near a wall, door, or other vertical surface. Use the masking tape to tape a 2-foot-long piece of paper on the wall where the child can easily reach it from a lying position.

2. Put on smocks. On each plate, pour a different color of paint. Have a wet rag and a dry rag available nearby for cleanup.

3. Have your child lie on their back with their feet toward the wall, then place both feet on the ground and lift their hips to form a bridge. Next, have them take one foot and, with their hips still in the air, step in the paint and use it to make a footprint on the paper on the wall. Switch and use the other foot. Guide them if necessary.

4. Have your child sit on the exercise ball and reach to the sides or down to get paint on their hands, then reach up on the paper to make handprints. Hold your child steady at the hips if needed.

5. Finally, have your child lie on their belly on the exercise ball and try an airplane position, but with their legs on the ground for support. They can reach down to the floor to get paint on their hands and then give high fives (and high tens) to the paper. Provide support for balance and safety as needed.

To make it easier: *If your child doesn't like getting paint on their hands or feet, they can use a paintbrush.*

To make it harder: *Get creative with the art and get into a plank position on the ball (with arms, belly, and chest on the ball, and knees off the floor) to paint.*

SKILLS
LEARNED

Gross Motor
Skills

Hand-Eye
Coordination

Fine Motor
Skills

Balloon Volleyball

Play volleyball without a court, a net, or even a volleyball! See who can get the highest score in this fun balloon game while helping your child work on motor skills such as balance and coordination. Mix it up by using a tennis racket or (clean) flyswatter to hit the balloon.

Age: 4+
Prep time: 5 minutes
Activity time: 15 to
30 minutes

MATERIALS

1 balloon, plus backups in case it pops

Masking tape

1 coin or other way to select who goes first

Tennis racket (optional)

Balance board (optional)

STEPS

1. Blow up a balloon.

2. Make a line with the masking tape in the middle of the room to create the "net." Stand in the middle of the room with one player on each side of the tape.

3. Flip a coin to select who goes first. The first player throws the balloon up and hits it over the masking tape, overhand or underhand, using one or both hands, to the other person.

4. Take turns hitting the balloon back and forth over the "net" and run around on your side to get the balloon.

5. When one player lets the balloon touch the ground, the other player gets a point. Play to a score of 5 or higher.

To make it easier: *Have your child simply focus on hitting the balloon up in the air 3 or 4 times without it touching the ground.*

To make it harder: *Play while standing on one foot, or even on a balance board. To work on oral motor skills, have your child help blow up the balloon.*

Paintbrush Water Writing

Kids love to paint! Out on your driveway, on the sidewalk, or on a chalk-board, let your child use a wet paintbrush to get artistic while working on their motor skills—all without getting too messy.

Age: 4+

Prep time: 5 minutes

Activity time: 20 minutes

MATERIALS

Bucket or large cup full of water

2 or 3 large paintbrushes

Chalk

STEPS

1. Get down on the ground on your belly with your child, dip a paintbrush in the water, and start writing letters with it. Begin with big letters, using your entire arm to write.

2. Next, have your child make the letters smaller, resting their forearm on the ground as needed, and focus on small wrist and finger movements to "paint" letters.

3. Reinforce letter formation by writing the letters in chalk first and then encouraging your child to trace them using the wet paintbrush.

To make it easier: *Write with the wet paintbrush on a chalkboard, or with chalk or markers on paper taped to a wall. Children under the age of 4 can "paint" shapes instead of letters.*

To make it harder: *See how many letters or words your child can write before the first letter dries up. Do this in the shade and the sun to see the difference.*

SKILLS
LEARNED

Gross Motor
Skills

Hand-Eye
Coordination

Fine Motor
Skills

Paper Soccer

Your child won't realize they're refining motor skills and hand-eye coordination—all they'll know is they're having fun playing a miniature game of "soccer" that doesn't require a field, a net, or even a soccer ball.

Age: 4+

Prep time: 5 minutes

Activity time:
10 minutes or more

MATERIALS

Masking tape or
small baskets

Piece of paper

STEPS

1. Using the masking tape or baskets, set up 2 goals on the floor no more than 4 feet apart.

2. Take the piece of paper and rip it in half, showing your child how to use a pincer grasp to pinch the top of the paper between the thumb and index finger of both hands, then rotate your wrists in opposite directions to rip.

3. Have your child rip the half sheet of paper into at least 4 smaller pieces.

4. Then have your child pick up one piece of paper with just one hand and crumple it into a small ball, using their fingers to roll it around and apply pressure.

5. Take the paper ball and place it midway between the two goals. Get down on your bellies.

6. Taking turns, try to flick the ball into the other person's goal until one person gets the desired number of points (5, 10, etc.).

To make it easier: *If your child tries to use two hands to crumple the paper, or places their hand on their body for more support, have them sit on their non-dominant hand and place the hand they're using up in the air as they crumple. If that's too much, have them lie on their belly and place their forearm on the floor but still use only one hand to crumple the paper.*

To make it harder: *Increase the distance between goals and have your child army-crawl while flicking the ball forward toward the goal.*

Cardboard Tube Marble Maze

Help your child get creative, problem-solve, and work on those fine motor skills by creating their own cool and interactive marble maze with household items.

Age: 4+

Prep time: 30 minutes

Activity time: 30 minutes

MATERIALS

Colored masking tape or duct tape

Empty toilet paper rolls

Empty paper towel rolls

Child scissors

Painter's tape

Marbles

Cardboard box, various cardboard scraps (optional)

Small container, such as an empty fresh fruit box

Plastic juice containers (optional)

Plastic cups (optional)

STEPS

1. Have your child pull off pieces of colored masking tape and wrap the tape around the cardboard rolls to decorate them and to connect the rolls. Encourage them not to let the tape bunch up.

2. While watching your child, let them use child scissors to cut the rolls in half lengthwise.

3. Show your child how to use the painter's tape to tape the cardboard tubes to clear wall space at various angles and distances. The goal is to create a maze for the marble, so when you drop it in at the top, it goes down through all the tubes. Test the design with marbles as you go to make sure it works. Use cardboard scraps as needed.

4. Place a container at the mouth of the last tube to catch the marble at the end.

5. Drop the marble in at the top and watch it go through the marble maze!

6. Let your child add more pieces, change the design of the maze, or just play with their creation.

To make it easier: *Have the adult construct the marble maze and simply allow the child to manipulate, pick up, and place the marble into the run.*

To make it harder: *For children age 5 or older, don't provide a model. Let them get creative with the activity.*

Training Camp Challenge

Welcome to boot camp! In this activity, your child must pay attention and follow directions in a training camp–style obstacle course to work on balance, coordination, and following verbal directions.

Age: 5+
Prep time: 15 minutes
Activity time: 20 minutes

MATERIALS

Masking tape

Pool noodle

2 chairs

Whistle (optional)

Timer (optional)

STEPS

1. Use the masking tape to mark the beginning and end of the obstacle course, at least 8 to 12 feet apart.

2. Halfway between the markers, hang the pool noodle between the 2 chairs, no higher than 6 inches off the floor.

3. Have your child start at one end of the obstacle course, then call out directions to them. If you want, blow the whistle to signal the start and stop of each action, and use the timer to time it. Examples of actions:

   - Run in place for 30 seconds.

   - Do 8 forward lunges, alternating legs with each lunge.

   - Army-crawl to the pool noodle.

   - Stand next to the pool noodle and jump over it sideways 6 times, back and forth, landing on two feet and starting again in a sideways position.

- Complete 10 jumping jacks.
- Do 6 military marches to the finish line. While marching forward, bend your left knee and cross your right hand over your body to touch the opposite knee, then repeat on the other side.

4. Demonstrate each movement if needed.

To make it easier: *Practice each step as a separate activity.*

To make it harder: *Add higher obstacles to jump over or new movements such as star jumps or side lunges.*

Chapter Four

Social-Emotional Skills

SOCIAL-EMOTIONAL DEVELOPMENT COVERS FIVE AREAS: SOCIAL relationships, communication abilities, play development, emotional regulation, and self-awareness. Social relationships and communication abilities develop first, as a child learns to engage with the world and other people. Play development is also a crucial stepping-stone, allowing children to explore new ideas and build skills such as social engagement, paying attention, and emotional regulation. As children age, they show increased self-awareness and awareness of others' emotions, which helps them collaboratively work with others.

The activities in this chapter are beneficial for any children with social-emotional differences, but they're also great for all kids, as they promote skills that are the basis of human engagement.

Funny Faces

Making silly faces has benefits! This activity helps your child show interest in joyful interactions, seek out your attention, and find ways to engage with you, as a foundation for communication and play.

Age: 1+
Prep time: 5 minutes
Activity time: 15 minutes

MATERIALS

Your faces!

STEPS

1. Find a quiet space without distractions. Have your child either lie on the floor or sit on your lap. If needed, use sensory strategies such as wrapping them in a blanket or body sock to help keep their attention.

2. Start using a very energetic and silly voice to gain your child's attention.

3. Add silly faces and basic actions such as sticking your tongue out, smiling, giggling, and making raspberry noises. Respond to their actions and change your voice volume, such as from a loud voice when commenting on their actions to a whisper when asking a question.

4. Provide deep pressure like big tickles (light-touch tickles can overstimulate), squeezes, or bouncing to help keep your child's attention.

To make it easier: *Adjust sensory input based on your child's preferences. Consider dimming the lights, lowering your voice, and limiting changes in facial expressions.*

To make it harder: *Move around the room so your child can follow your face as you engage. Imitate the faces and sounds your child makes and see if your child will imitate them back!*

Tickles and Hugs

Use this simple game of tickles and/or hugs to work on building shared attention, anticipation, and nonverbal communication.

Age: 1+
Activity time: 10 minutes

No materials are needed for this activity.

STEPS

1. On a safe, cushioned surface, with your child lying on their back, tickle their belly.

2. Wait for a response. Does your child smile or look toward you? Do they pull your hands onto their belly or otherwise communicate they want more?

3. If they like it, turn it into an anticipation game, making your voice more animated, going either slow or quick to tickle them. Change it up so your child is excited to see what you'll do next!

4. Tickle different body parts and wait to see how your child communicates they want more. Do they lift an arm or place your hand on their leg? If you pair tickling with the word "tickle" or another easy sound, do they imitate it when asking for more?

5. Pay close attention to your child's body cues and stop as soon as they're done or overwhelmed. This activity is meant to help them engage with you, not to overwhelm them.

To make it easier: *Use intermittent hugs or deep pressure if they're sensitive to touch.*

To make it harder: *Help them understand body parts by asking them to either lift certain body parts to get tickled or say what certain body parts are as you tickle them.*

Joining In

What's your child's favorite activity? The focus here is to join them in it! Sit back and observe your child's interests and thought processes, then join them, imitating their play actions and using toys the way they do. You'll expand on these actions to entice your child to engage socially.

Age: 1+
Prep time: 5 minutes
Activity time: 15 minutes

MATERIALS

Highly preferred toys or objects (optional)

STEPS

1. In any location or place of interest for your child, sit and observe what interests your child. Is it how the light comes through the blinds? Do they like spinning—watching a ceiling fan, spinning their bodies, or spinning the wheels on a toy car?

2. Do some detective work, breaking down the parts of the activity to understand why your child might be interested. What sensory experiences seem to interest or please them? How does your child interact with these experiences? Does this help your child calm down? Provide consistent and expected reactions? Bring joy, pleasure, and other "good" feelings?

3. Sit on the floor next to them and imitate their actions—such as spinning the wheels on the same car (or a different car), taking turns spinning your bodies, or watching the light or fan—to join their world.

4. Use these interests to expand on back-and-forth social engagement:

   - Consider playful "obstruction," such as placing your hand over their toy car's wheels or turning the fan off or up.

- Build on interactions by acting as if your hand is stuck in that position.

- Wait to see how your child responds and communicates (verbally and nonverbally) for you to remove your hand from the wheel or switch. Continue with this playful approach if they enjoy it.

To make it easier: *If your child becomes upset or dysregulated, step back and focus just on joining in rather than working on expanding play and communication exchanges. Always acknowledge your child's feelings and try to talk about their emotions if possible.*

To make it harder: *Depending on your child's communication abilities, ask questions to understand their play ideas further. See examples provided in Tea Party (page 119).*

Working through Big Feelings

Use this activity in the moment, when big feelings arise. It works on providing positive feedback for any emotions—no matter how big they are—and finding solutions to work through these big feelings.

Age: 2+
Prep time: As needed
Activity time: As needed

No materials are needed for this activity.

STEPS

1. When a situation leads to big feelings, step back and assess the situation. How can you support your child in the moment? Can your child use communication in the moment to discuss big feelings, or is a sensory strategy a better choice?

2. If your child is unable to communicate or problem-solve in the moment, try sensory tools, such as Sensory Strategy Cards (page 52), a Sensory Calming Bin (page 30), Sight and Sound Jars (page 39), a Crash Mat (see page 27 to build your own), etc.

3. If your child *is* able to work through their feelings in the moment, have an open discussion. Comments might include: "We all experience some big feelings." "It's okay to feel these feelings and everyone has their own ways of dealing with them." "Can you tell me what emotions you're feeling right now?" "Do you know why you're feeling this way?"

4. Work toward finding simple solutions for the big emotions, whether that means using the sensory tools, inviting your child to stomp their feet or rip paper, or even playing a game of catch to help their body reorganize and calm.

I Can't Reach It!

Work on social problem-solving by placing play items slightly out of reach and having your child either describe or gesture ways to work together to retrieve the desired item.

Age: 2+
Prep time: 5 minutes
Activity time: 20 minutes

MATERIALS

Stuffed toy or another desired item

High counter or cabinet

1 or 2 containers

Safe item to stand on, such as a child's stool

Item to help reach for the object, such as a grabber toy or tongs

STEPS

1. Place the stuffed toy on a high counter or cabinet, and place the containers in front of the toy to increase the communication needed to get to the toy.

2. Have available the stool, grabber, and any other items that might be used as part of this problem-solving activity.

3. Call your child over and ask for help, pretending you can't reach and are uncertain how to get the toy down.

4. Think of ways to work together and problem-solve with your child. Ask, "How can we get it down?" "What can we use?" "What about using this?"

5. Encourage working together using playful obstruction ideas—perhaps the stool isn't tall enough or the grabber doesn't work. Work together to "fix" the problem or find alternative solutions to reach for the toy.

To make it easier: *Offer suggestions and choices for working together to get the toy down.*

To make it harder: *Expand on social problem-solving skills by stepping up the challenge, such as fixing toys or finding objects. Refer to the Roadblock! activity (page 112).*

Breath and Heartbeat Listening

Invite your child to jump up and down, sit, and feel their heartbeat and breathing as a way to bring self-awareness to their body. This is also a simple strategy to calm their body.

Age: 2+
Prep time: 5 minutes
Activity time: 10 minutes

MATERIALS

Yoga mat or blanket

STEPS

1. Have your child jump up and down for at least 30 seconds.

2. Have your child stop and sit on a yoga mat or blanket on the floor.

3. Have your child close their eyes and place their hands over their heart to feel and listen.

4. Have your child place their hands over their chest to feel their lungs breathing.

5. Discuss with your child what and how they're feeling. What else do they notice?

To make it easier: *Use Breathing Ball (page 35) to increase your child's awareness of their breathing and count the number of breaths.*

To make it harder: *Use mental imagery related to deep breaths to work on controlling the number of breaths in the moment. (See A Scene of Senses on page 126.)*

The Face in the Mirror

What faces go with different emotions? This activity is designed to help your child learn to recognize these telling facial expressions in themselves and others.

Age: 2+
Prep time: 5 minutes
Activity time: 15 minutes

MATERIALS

2 small stand-up mirrors, or a larger mirror to share

Paper and crayons or markers (optional)

STEPS

1. Place the stand-up mirrors on a table or the floor, or stand in front of a larger mirror together.

2. Start with a simple face. Ask your child to make a happy face or smile, or have your child identify your simple happy facial expression.

3. Together, explore different facial expressions for angry, upset, frustrated, worried, scared, surprised, etc. Vary the facial expressions by either calling out faces for them to make or having your child guess the face you're making.

4. Add additional feelings and explore subtleties, such as anxious versus scared, and so on.

To make it easier: *Focus on basic emotions such as happy, sad, and mad.*

To make it harder: *For children age 3 and older, have them choose or identify feelings, look in the mirror, make the associated face, and then draw a self-portrait using that emotion.*

Feelings Drawings

Use this activity to build on Body-Level Messages (page 58) and Map My Feelings (page 56). This activity uses drawings like the ones in Body-Level Messages, but it focuses on identifying daily situations that can lead to certain big feelings.

Age: 3+
Prep time: 15 minutes
Activity time: 30 minutes

MATERIALS

4 or 5 sheets of paper

Pencil or pen

Images from online or a magazine (optional)

Scissors (optional)

Glue (optional)

Laminator (optional)

STEPS

1. On each sheet of paper, write, or have your child write, "I feel _____ when . . ." Leave space underneath to draw or glue printed images (if using).

2. Create a sheet for the following emotions: angry, sad, frustrated, worried, and happy.

3. For each emotion, have your child think of situations that can lead to this emotion, such as "I feel mad when my shoes get soggy on the wet grass," "I feel worried when I have to talk in front of a big group of people," or "I feel sad when a friend says unkind words to me."

4. Help your child cut out and glue on images to match the emotions if desired. Laminate the pages if desired.

To make it easier: *Provide examples of different situations for your child to match to associated emotions. For example, "How do you feel when you get a letter in the mail?"*

To make it harder: *Discuss these big feelings in the moment (see Working through Big Feelings, page 102).*

Group Painting

Let your child work with friends or siblings to decide what items to use, who will do what, and how to work together on a collaborative work of art. Activities like this build on cooperative play skills—which will come in handy throughout life.

Age: 3+
Prep time: 10 minutes
Activity time: 30 minutes

MATERIALS

Easel paper or large (at least 16-by-20-inch) drawing paper

Washable paints in various colors

Paintbrushes

Smocks

Pencil

Cup for water

Paper towels or rag

STEPS

1. Place the paper on a table or easel, with the paints and paintbrushes nearby. Put on smocks.

2. Have your child use the pencil to draw a large circle, nearly as large as the paper (or draw it for them).

3. Have your child and their friends decide together on what colors to use, which paintbrushes are needed, who will fill the cup with water, and who will get the towels.

4. Direct the children to paint in the circle using agreed-upon patterns or colors. Can they work together to fill the circle?

5. Let them work this out together. Watch who takes which roles. Who leads or follows? Who keeps an open mind to different opinions? Who is willing to compromise? As needed, help them ask open-ended questions, reflect on big feelings, and take turns in different roles.

To make it easier: *Use just one color to color in the circle, focusing on covering all the "white spots."*

To make it harder: *Have the kids create a painted scene together. Let them decide together on a picture and work together to add different components, with you nearby to help support a dialogue.*

Plastic Eiffel Tower

How wide and tall can your young architect build an Eiffel Tower made of plastic party cups? Have one or more friends join to problem-solve together and gather items needed to complete the tower without letting it fall down.

Age: 3+
Prep time: 5 minutes
Activity time: 30 minutes

MATERIALS

20 or more plastic party cups

STEPS

1. Direct your child and a friend to use the cups to build a tower as wide and as high as possible.

2. Let them problem-solve specific placement of the cups.

3. Encourage collaboration and idea sharing by asking guiding questions:

   - "How can you make the widest and tallest tower?"

   - "In which direction might it be best to place the cups?"

   - "Oh, that looks like a tricky spot. I wonder what your friend thinks about that idea."

4. Provide support when there are differences in ideas, reassuring the kids it's okay to have different opinions. Provide support by acknowledging the strengths and weaknesses of each idea presented by each child to encourage them to work together to compromise.

5. As they work to complete the tower, watch and listen. What do they do well together? What are the biggest issues you see? Are they able to improve communication and work as a team? End their tower-building session with praise and high fives for their awesome work.

Fine Motor Skills

Visual Spatial Skills

To make it easier: *Let your child build the tower with an adult, or have one child lead the first round, then switch roles for the second round.*

To make it harder: *Incorporate different cup sizes or different objects to increase the cognitive and problem-solving demands and further challenge group thinking skills.*

SKILLS LEARNED

Self-Awareness

Emotional Regulation

Play Development

Social Relationships

Communication

Cloudy with a Chance of Sunshine

Weather can be like emotions! In this activity, your child will learn to think of changes in the weather as a way to understand changes in emotions throughout the day, or even within a short time frame. It's a great way to check in with your child first thing in the morning.

Age: 3+
Prep time: 10 minutes
Activity time: 15 minutes

MATERIALS

Printed pictures of basic weather conditions or paper and crayons to draw them (optional)

Images of facial expressions (optional)

STEPS

1. Talk with your child about various weather conditions, such as sunny, cloudy, windy, rainy, snowy, stormy, etc. With older children, you can talk about concepts such as hail, tornadoes, hurricanes, etc.

2. Now talk about various emotions. Can your child relate an emotion to different weather conditions? For example, if you say "sad" or "crying," they might connect that with rain. Prompt them if needed—perhaps you can ask, "How does a sunny day make you feel?" See if they can independently associate different feelings with different weather conditions.

3. This can also be used as a group activity. Go around the group and ask each child which weather condition they associate with right now and have the group try to guess the emotion they might be feeling.

4. Use weather patterns to bring up various conversations regarding emotions:

- Explain to your child how thinking about weather conditions can help them understand their emotions.

- Discuss how weather patterns are sometimes hard to change (like a bad mood!), or can change very rapidly (like sudden joy when something awesome happens).

- Explain that everyone experiences different emotions and that these emotions do not define who they are. Discuss how they can use various strategies to help work through big feelings.

To make it easier: *Pair weather pictures to pictures of different faces.*

To make it harder: *Expand to other themes and concepts, such as music or animals. Can your child independently link these representations to their own emotions?*

SKILLS LEARNED

Self-Awareness

Emotional Regulation

Play Development

Social Relationships

Communication

Visual Spatial Skills

Roadblock!

Build on higher-level social problem-solving skills by creating a "road-block." This activity challenges your child with changes to play ideas or obstacles as part of play. Help your child work through the challenge by offering suggestions that may not work or might require alternatives. The goal is not to frustrate your child but to expand their thinking. A literal roadblock during a car game is used as an example, but you can create any sort of figurative roadblock you wish!

Age: 3+
Prep time: 10 minutes
Activity time: 20 minutes

MATERIALS

Toy cars or other vehicles

Blocks or ropes

STEPS

1. Let your child create a play idea with toy cars, such as having the cars go down a road, over a bridge, or through a car wash. As you play together, use the blocks to introduce obstacles slowly, such as a construction roadblock, railroad crossing gate, etc. Start with simple, open-ended questions, such as:

    *   "Why can't we go over the bridge?"

    *   "How did the car get stuck?"

    *   "What's blocking the car?"

    Slowly provide more support as needed to work through the problem together.

2. Offer suggestions that "don't make sense," so your child can be the smart one and offer alternatives and logic-based solutions, which allows them to use a combination of shared and independent thinking.

3. Expand on the pretend play idea—perhaps the bridge has a hole and needs to be fixed. What items can your child find to help fix it so the cars can cross again?

To make it easier: *Provide support to set up the play theme. Keep it simple, such as using a block to prevent the car from going down the road and figuring out how to get the block "unstuck" from the road. Provide as much emotional support as needed to help your child remain regulated.*

To make it harder: *Let your child make the roadblocks and offer various silly and not-so-silly solutions to help solve the problem!*

Wheel of Coping Skills

Spin the Wheel of Coping Skills to determine a strategy or technique to help your child cope with big feelings and work toward being able to remain calm or calm down in various situations.

Age: 3+
Prep time: 30 minutes
Activity time: 20 minutes

MATERIALS

2 paper plates

Scissors

Paper fastener/brad

Markers

STEPS

1. From one paper plate, cut out a small triangle about one-eighth the size of the plate, spanning from the middle toward the edge (before the rim/bumps of the plate's edge).

2. Take a second plate and attach it behind the first plate using a paper fastener.

3. Rotate the open window from the top plate into various eighth sections and write different coping strategies in each area that typically work for your child. Here are some examples:

  - Take 4 or 5 deep breaths.

  - Do a full-body relaxation.

  - Go for a walk or run.

  - Play Map My Feelings (page 56).

  - Go to your Sensory Safe Space (page 25).

  - Read a book, draw, listen to music.

  - Use sensory tools, such as the Sensory Calming Bin (page 30) or Sensory Strategy Cards (page 52).

  - Ask for help.

4. Have your child decorate the wheel, as desired.

5. Describe different situations and invite your child to close their eyes and turn the wheel. Wherever it lands, ask if they can use this specific coping strategy in that moment. For example, when frustrated, your child might benefit from a walk or run, but they can identify that this strategy may not work at school, so they might need to spin the wheel to find another appropriate tool.

6. This can be added to your child's Sensory Calming Bin (page 30), or be used whenever big feelings arise.

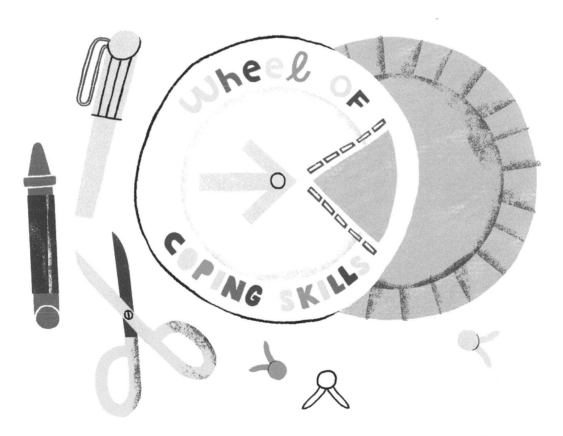

Self-Awareness	Emotional Regulation	Interoception	Communication
	♥		💬

Whole-Body Relaxation

Here's a great exercise for whole-body relaxation, with step-by-step directions for your child to tighten and then loosen all their muscles to relax and increase awareness of body reactions.

Age: 3+
Prep time: 5 minutes
Activity time: 10 minutes

MATERIALS

Yoga mat or blanket

STEPS

1. Have your child lie on the floor on a yoga mat or blanket.

2. Instruct your child to let their arms relax at their sides, spread out in a comfortable way, and close their eyes.

3. Direct them to tighten and squeeze the muscles in their feet and curl their toes. Have them hold for a count of 5 but breathe regularly. After 5 seconds, they can relax their feet and toes.

4. Then have them move up their body doing the same thing: squeezing then releasing the muscles in their legs, belly, arms, and hands, each for a count of 5. Have them continue, lifting their shoulders up to their ears, and then moving up to their face, tightening their jaw and scrunching their face.

5. Once everything is released, have them relax as light as a feather on the mat.

6. Repeat as needed.

To make it easier: *Use guided imagery to tighten different body parts, such as telling them to tighten their belly "as hard as a rock" and make their hands into fists "like you're popping a balloon."*

Homemade Stress Ball

Let your child make their own stress balls! Keep a bunch on hand so they have access to this useful tool in different situations—it can even double as a fidget toy for times they have to sit for an extended period.

Age: 3+
Prep time: 5 minutes
Activity time: 15 minutes

MATERIALS

1 or more colors of play dough (see page 166 to make your own)

Party balloons

Permanent marker (optional)

STEPS

1. Have your child use their hands to roll out the play dough into one long snake shape, or a few smaller snake shapes.

2. Stretch the balloon opening as wide as possible so your child can stuff in the play dough snake shapes.

3. Have your child press the balloon to get the air out. Tie a knot at the end.

4. Add a face to the stress ball, if desired.

5. Let your child explore squishing and squeezing the ball. Have it available as needed.

To make it easier: *If your child is unable to pay attention long enough or has fine motor challenges, create the stress ball for them and keep it handy as a regulation tool when needed.*

To make it harder: *Talk with your child about how squeezing the ball makes them feel, and discuss times they can use it.*

Cardboard Adventures

Take out some old cardboard boxes and packaging and other craft materials and start building houses, forts, and more. Sure, it's fun, but it also helps develop high-level abstract thinking. This activity focuses on creativity, but suggestions for construction and assistance with working on higher-level social emotional skills are also included.

Age: 3+
Prep time: 20 minutes
Activity time: 30 minutes

MATERIALS

2 or 3 large cardboard boxes

4 or 5 medium and small cardboard boxes

Masking tape

Marker or crayons

Ribbons, stickers, and/or other craft materials

Paper plates

Ice pop sticks

Paper towel rolls or toilet paper rolls

STEPS

1. Provide your child with the materials and invite them to build something of their choosing: a house, fort, car, pirate ship, dinosaur cove—whatever!

2. Provide as much or as little assistance as they need to connect boxes using tape. Let your child design and decorate.

3. Offer some pretend play ideas to build on your child's abstract and representational thinking:

  *   Suggest substituting one item to represent another, such as a paper plate to represent a steering wheel, connected ice pop sticks as the mast for a sail, or two connected toilet paper rolls to act as binoculars.

  *   Explore imaginary concepts, asking your child what they see out in the ocean or through their binoculars.

  *   Discuss their plan, such as where they're going, what they might do there, who they might see, why they're going, and how they plan to get there.

Tea Party

A simple tea party can help your child create and expand on new play ideas and become more independent during play. Step back and let your child take the lead, but also provide supportive comments to build on new ideas and expand emotional themes.

Age: 4+

Prep time: 10 minutes

Activity time: 20 minutes

MATERIALS

Tea party set or plastic cups, plates, and utensils

Table or mat

STEPS

1. Take turns being the tea party host. Give your child the opportunity to set up and offer play ideas.

2. Be patient as your child takes the lead. Determine what your child's next play steps might involve. If they're on a roll, follow their lead. If they seem stuck, helpful comments can encourage your child to begin to initiate their own ideas and develop a play theme. You might say: "My tea is cold. I wonder what we can do."

3. Try building further on play by asking questions such as "When should I check the water for the tea?" or "How is the tea made?"

4. Add new ideas to the story with different food items, or make shifts in the story line to work on flexible thinking, such as saying, "My tummy is full. I can't have more tea!" Then provide guidance on what can be done next: "You think we should clean up? Good idea!"

5. Get creative with your child and introduce and involve a variety of different emotions, then act out these emotions during play. For example, you might say, "Oh my gosh, your friend didn't show up for your tea party! How does that make you feel?" Or, "We just spilled the tea! Now what?"

Turn Which Way?

Wearing a blindfold is disorienting, but you'll provide your child with directions to navigate through a small and safe obstacle course. Then switch and have your child provide directions to you, to work on their direction-following, attention, and teamwork skills!

Age: 4+

Prep time: 15 minutes

Activity time: 20 minutes

MATERIALS

5 or 6 cones

3 or 4 Hula-Hoops or ropes made into circle shapes

Household items: 4 chairs, bench or step stool, 2 pool noodles or something to jump over

Masking tape

Tunnel or cardboard box large enough for your child to crawl through

Blindfold, such as a sleeping mask or bandanna

STEPS

1. Set up the obstacle course according to your child's abilities. Here are some ideas:

   - Spread the cones in a straight line.

   - Place the Hula-Hoops flat on the ground in a staggered line, or prop them up vertically with support from other household items and masking tape.

   - Place two sets of two chairs at an even distance, with a pool noodle between each set of chairs no more than 6 inches off the ground, or just set up something to jump over.

   - Place a stool or bench in the middle of the area.

   - Place a tunnel on the ground, or use a large cardboard box opened at the top and bottom for a makeshift tunnel.

   - Place a blindfold on your child and say, "You're going to complete an obstacle course. I will describe the steps you need to do, using words to direct you. I won't help you unless you need me to."

2. Tailor the directions to the child's age and ability, such as directions to turn (left or right, or turning one way or the other way), walk forward or backward, turn around, crawl under objects, pick up feet over objects, or move around an item.

3. After your child completes the course, switch roles and put on the blindfold. Have your child describe the directions with words and descriptions.

4. Reflect together on the experience.

   * Ask your child how it felt describing directions and being blindfolded.

   * How does this obstacle course make your child work on trusting others?

   * What was easy to describe and what was hard to describe?

To make it easier: *Let your child see the obstacle course before completing it.*

To make it harder: *For children age 5 or older, ask what the importance of the activity was. Did they learn any strategies that might be helpful for other daily routines?*

Puppet Show

Use puppets to role-play situations that make your child feel frustrated, upset, or fearful, such as sharing toys, adjusting to a schedule change, or going to a crowded store. Incorporate fine motor components by making puppets from brown bags and expressing different emotions on the puppets' faces.

Age: 4+
Prep time: 30 minutes
Activity time: 30 minutes

MATERIALS

6 or more brown paper lunch bags

Markers or crayons

Printed pictures of faces (optional)

Glue (optional)

Googly eyes (optional)

STEPS

1. Identify 5 or 6 emotions, such as happy, sad, upset, frustrated, angry, scared, and worried.

2. Have your child draw faces (with googly eyes, if using) on the base of the bag so that when you stick your hand in the opening, the fold in the base of the bag will move like a mouth. (You can also provide printed pictures for your child to copy or glue onto the different puppets' faces.)

3. Have your child identify 3 situations where they might feel the emotions on one of the puppets' faces.

4. Act out those situations with the puppet. For example:

   • Act out another puppet taking a pretend toy from the Frustrated puppet. Have your child use the Frustrated puppet to talk about their feelings in the moment and any other emotions that come up.

- Have your child use the Upset puppet while you act out getting ready for a favorite activity but then change the plan at the last minute. How does the Upset puppet act in the moment? How does the puppet's body feel and how can we help the Upset puppet work through those big feelings?

To make it easier: *Use puppets or other toys you already have in your home. Pick simple emotions and just work on acting out these feelings rather than associating them with specific situations.*

To make it harder: *Let your child take the lead, creating situations and working through associated feelings.*

Superheroes

Who's your superhero? Let your child choose or make up their own superhero and theme to work on imaginative play and sequencing ideas. How long can your child stretch the story theme and stick to the play idea while introducing various concepts and logically connecting their thoughts? Do this in a park or a small room—just bring your imaginations!

Age: 4+

Prep time: 15 minutes

Activity time: 30 minutes

MATERIALS

Play wands or household items to represent other superhero action items

Blocks, playhouses, or Legos (optional)

Cape and other super-hero clothing (optional)

STEPS

1. Together, discuss a superhero your child wants to "be" and a situation to role-play.

2. Have your child gather items they want to use as part of play and bring them to the setting where their adventure will take place.

3. Let your child set up the items and initiate ideas.

4. Help your child with guiding questions. For example:

   - **Comment on their actions:** "Oh, wow! That was a big kick to knock down the tower!" Or, "You flew right over that bad guy."

   - **Help build on the play:** "What was your superhero's plan when they pushed down the tower?" Or, "Wow—you're strong. Why did you use that wand to fight off the bad guy? What powers does it have?"

   - **Expand and reflect on ideas:** "I'm confused. How was your superhero able to get to the bad guys when we were just at their house?"

5. The goal is for your child to weave together all their ideas, perhaps starting at the superhero's house, then getting in the superhero's car, driving to the bad guys, and defeating the bad guys. Don't take over—let your child introduce the theme and use the suggested comments and questions to expand the play and create connections between their ideas to help them create a story line.

To make it easier: *Just focus on building pretend play ideas within a specific scene, such as how to defeat the bad guys.*

To make it harder: *Let your child go as deep as they wish with a variety of themes and work together with friends to negotiate ideas and create complex play scenarios.*

A Scene of Senses

The broad field of mindfulness can be used in many beneficial ways for children and adults alike. When experiencing big feelings, your child can use this mindfulness activity to imagine a favorite scene or mental picture, focus on their senses and associated feelings, and calm their body and mind.

Age: 4+
Prep time: 5 minutes
Activity time: 15 minutes

MATERIALS

Calming music (optional)

STEPS:

1. Sit together in a quiet place. Have your child pick a place or scene they find enjoyable and relaxing. Provide suggestions if needed.

2. Let's say your child is imagining the beach. Have your child describe two things they *see*, like the color of the sunset or the shape of the waves.

3. Have your child describe two things they *hear*, like crashing waves or grass on the dunes rustling in the wind.

4. Have your child describe two things they *feel*, like sand between their toes or a smooth, hard shell.

5. Have your child describe two things they *smell*, like the salty smell of water or the scent of sunscreen.

6. Have your child describe two things they *taste*, like the taste of salt water or their favorite beach snack.

7. Have your child describe how they're *moving*, like being pushed by a wave or doing a cartwheel in the sand.

8. Have your child describe their *body positioning,* like being buried up to their neck in sand or resting under a heavy beach towel.

9. Have your child describe two or more *body responses,* like enjoying the cold ocean water or feeling delight at seeing the waves.

10. When possible, guide your child with leading questions, or have them go through all the imagery they have conjured up to work on calming their body in the moment or after experiencing big feelings.

To make it easier: *Play soothing music and go over only a few senses. Provide support and choices as needed.*

To make it harder: *After doing the activity, have your child break down the activity and discuss parts that were and were not successful.*

Cup/Brain Overflow

In this activity, your child will use a cup to represent their brain and fill it with various items that represent struggles, worries, or other challenges. When does it overflow? This overflow illustrates the times when your child can no longer hold it together and might have a meltdown. Use this activity as an opportunity to learn what your child's worries are, as you discuss how situations can build and which strategies can help remove items from the cup and prevent it from overflowing.

Age: 5+

Prep time: 15 minutes

Activity time: 15 minutes

MATERIALS

3 or 4 different-size cups, ranging from a small drinking cup to a large container

Scooper or large spoon

Batches of small objects, such as large beads, pom-poms, small figurines, small rocks, marbles

STEPS

1. For each object, have your child identify a situation to be represented by that object. For example, your child may choose marbles to represent homework and pom-poms to represent loud sounds. Use as many items as they wish.

2. Discuss each worry, struggle, or challenge as they place a scoop of the representative item into the cup.

3. How many items will it take to fill the cup? Explain to your child how this represents their brain, which can only hold so much, and that when too many worries get into their head, it's hard to hold it together and it overflows. Explain that this can result in a meltdown.

4. Explore with different-size cups and see how many "worries" it takes to overflow them.

5. Discuss situations that may present the same worries but can lead to different types of reactions. A great example is how your child might have a big cup to hold all their big worries at school, but when they come home a single misplaced shoe could make it overflow.

6. Tie this issue into the different sensory and social-emotional strategies discussed in this book (Sensory Safe Space/Hideout [page 25], Chew and Chill [page 26], Sensory Calming Bin [page 30], Breathing Ball [page 35], Sight and Sound Jars [page 39], Sensory Strategy Cards [page 52]), or other strategies you have found helpful. Using those strategies, how many worries can your child take out of the cup? Do new strategies need to be added to help remove more worries?

To make it easier: *Add sticky notes to each batch of objects to help your child remember which worry or other challenge it represents.*

To make it harder: *Talk about things that might make the size of their metaphorical cup change in a day, such as being tired, being sick, changes in routine, and so forth. Work with your child to recognize signs of changes to their body discussed in the Map My Feelings (page 56) and Feelings Drawings (page 106) activities. This will increase their self-awareness, allowing them to turn to helpful regulation strategies, or take needed breaks to prevent brain overflows.*

How Does That Make You Feel?

This activity provides various situations that let your child explore their emotions and how a friend or other person might have a different point of view. Take on different roles. How might your child's reaction affect another child?

Age: 5+
Prep time: 10 minutes
Activity time: 30 minutes

MATERIALS

Favorite toy characters or puppets

Imaginary characters (optional)

STEPS

1. Have your child initiate a favorite play idea with use of toy characters or puppets.

2. During play, introduce actions to elicit emotion, such as taking a toy from one of their characters, or having one character be unkind to another.

3. Through use of play, discuss how your child feels and how the character, or other person, might feel. Questions or comments may include:

   - **Point out the reaction:** "Look how sad the dog is! His head is hanging down!"

   - **Ask why:** "Why do you think the dog is so sad? Oh, because the owl took his bone?"

   - **Let your child consider other perspectives:** "The owl looks the same way the dog does. How do you think the owl is feeling? Why is the owl feeling this way?"

4. Provide play examples, and after an action takes place, instead of your child describing what they see, have them "step into" this character's "shoes."

- Ask your child how they would feel as this character when a toy is taken away or they do not get a turn.

- Talk about why the character took a certain action, especially if it is different from your child's idea. Discuss how all people have different interests and ideas and the reasons we consider everyone's ideas to work together.

To make it easier: *Have your child identify the other character's emotions in a particular situation.*

To make it harder: *Together, explore a variety of different and more complex or subtle emotions.*

Big Deal or Little Deal

Situations can be a big deal or a little deal, depending on the scenario and impact. Use this activity to teach your child how to explore their responses to see if their reactions match the situation.

Age: 5+
Prep time: 5 minutes
Activity time: 20 minutes

MATERIALS

Piece of paper

Crayons or markers

STEPS

1. Invite your child to draw a line and add a number scale from 1 to 10.

2. Label number 1 as a little deal, number 5 as a medium deal, and number 10 as a big deal. Your child can draw associated faces/emotions for the numbers if they wish.

3. Talk with your child about what makes some things a little deal versus a big deal. For example:

   - **Little deal:** A slight nuisance, causes only small changes in plans, has a short-term impact.

   - **Big deal:** Has a long-term impact, hard to get over quickly, makes big changes, can lead to big feelings.

4. Discuss situations that might fall into each category. For example:

   - **Little deal:** Bad weather means no outdoor play.

   - **Medium deal:** A sibling is unkind.

   - **Big deal:** You get a big injury, or a family member is ill.

5. Use the number line to rate different situations beyond just little, medium, or big. The goal is to help your child build sensitivity and perspective for dealing with various situations.

To make it easier: *Provide support and examples for your child to categorize situations as little deals or big deals.*

To make it harder: *Ask your child to think about how they respond to certain situations. Can they rate their response as a little, medium, or big response, or find a number on the scale that it matches? Does their "response" number match the number on the line? If not, discuss strategies they can use to react more appropriately.*

Flexible Minds

Help your child learn to cope with small changes to their routines. Board games are used as an example here, but you can practice these skills in many ways, like tweaking a daily routine.

Age: 5+
Prep time: 15 minutes
Activity time: 20 minutes

MATERIALS

Board game of choice (Connect 4, Chutes and Ladders, etc.)

STEPS

1. Set up the game and follow the rules as your family typically plays for the first round.

2. For the second round, change the rules. For example, with Connect 4, you might say that to win the round, someone must get five pieces in a row instead of four. Start with smaller changes and work toward bigger ones.

3. Provide support for any big feelings. Discuss how the activity makes your child feel. What might they need to do to calm their body, such as taking deep breaths or stating the problem? Provide compromises as needed.

4. Discuss with your child why the rules are being changed—so they can learn to work through problems and try new ways of doing things.

To make it easier: *If you change an idea and your child has a hard time remaining regulated, don't push. Just discuss these feelings.*

To make it harder: *Try this strategy with daily routines or play. If your child showers after dinner, encourage them to shower before dinner.*

Chapter Five

Cognitive and Visual Processing Skills

COGNITIVE AND VISUAL PROCESSING SKILLS PLAY a huge role in development—they provide the foundation for reading, writing, motor skills, play skills, critical thinking skills, and more. Examples of visual processing include hand-eye coordination, visual discrimination (the ability to identify details such as shape, size, and color), visual memory (the ability to recall what we've seen), and visual spatial skills (the ability to understand where things are in relation to each other). Examples of cognitive skills include imitating actions, short- and long-term memory, paying and shifting attention, safety awareness, and executive function (initiating, planning, sequencing, and organizing ideas). The activities in this chapter will help your child learn and use strategies to put these important skills into action as part of play and other daily routines.

Mirror Mirror

Mirror Mirror is a great game to have your child work on building relationships and strengthening imitation skills. This also helps develop visual memory skills and coordination. Start as the leader—and when your child is ready, let them lead.

Age: 1+
Prep time: 5 minutes
Activity time: 10 minutes

MATERIALS

Drawn pictures of positions to imitate (optional)

STEPS

1. Perform basic actions such as smiling, waving, clapping, or sticking out your tongue, and invite your child to imitate each one.

2. If your child is over 2, attempt more challenging actions such as running, jumping, or making silly faces.

3. If your child is over 3, try even more challenging actions such as yoga poses, balancing on one foot, or different animal walks.

To make it easier: *Provide pictures and verbal directions to break down the steps for your child to imitate.*

To make it harder: *With children over age 2, introduce an action and have them wait 30 seconds before repeating it. To make it even harder, have them engage in a different activity between seeing the action and trying to imitate it. For children over age 3, use a series of two or more actions to imitate.*

SKILLS LEARNED	Attention	Shared Engagement	Communication	Play Development	Touch

Water Chatter

This is a great way to cool off as you engage in an interactive game to work on imitation and communication skills by describing actions as part of play. Set up a safe water-filled area to play in or with, such as a bathtub, kiddie pool, water table, or sink, and use a variety of household items as toys.

Age: 1+

Prep time: 5 minutes

Activity time: 15 minutes

MATERIALS

Water toys: toy boats, rubber ducks, etc.

Measuring cups or other measuring containers

Items to pour water: milk jugs, buckets, etc.

STEPS

1. Fill the bathtub or other area with lukewarm water up to a safe height. Make sure your child is secured safely if necessary, and don't leave them unattended.

2. Add the water toys and other play items.

3. Let your child begin to explore the play items. If needed, show them how to engage with the toys.

4. Talk about what you're doing as part of play; describe your actions and compare things: "Now I'm pouring the water." "That's a big splash! This is a little splash."

5. Build on play skills by modeling actions such as pushing the boat or having the duck fly, and build on the play with open-ended questions, such as "Where is the duck flying?" or "Where is the boat going?" The goal is for your child to take the lead, create their own ideas, and begin to connect ideas in a sequence as part of play.

6. Encourage your child to respond to your questions and make comments on their own actions.

What's That Sound?

Use recorded sounds from online videos, record sounds on your phone, or make the sounds yourself! Have your child identify what makes that sound. This activity will help your child learn to pay attention to sounds, follow simple directions, and make basic motor actions.

Age: 1+
Prep time: 5 minutes
Activity time: 10 minutes

MATERIALS

Recordings of different sounds, which might include a fire truck, a barking dog, a knock on the door, pots banging, rain falling—get creative!

STEPS

1. Play one sound.

2. Ask your child, "What's that sound?" Use an excited voice and repeat the sound if needed.

3. Once your child identifies the sound, model actions that the thing making the sound might do, or ask your child to model the action.

To make it easier: *Have your child respond to the location of the sound. If your child is just beginning to speak, work on bringing your child's attention to the sound and then to you when you ask the question. Use pictures for your child to point to, or let them pick from a choice of 2 or 3 pictures.*

To make it harder: *Have your child make noises and you guess what it is.*

Bounce, Push, Crash

Is your child often on the go but has a hard time focusing? Or conversely, does your child have low energy, making it hard to wake up their body to play? Try this activity to provide heavy work and deep pressure to your child's body. Engaging in activities like this that involve increased input, pressure, and pushing/pulling motions can help calm or wake up the body for play or other activities.

Age: 1+, depending on your child's motor skills and safety of task

Prep time: 5 minutes

Activity time: 5 or more minutes, as needed, to "prepare" and transition to other activities

MATERIALS

Note: These are just suggestions. Use what is appropriate for your child's size and needs.

Exercise ball

Laundry basket full of items

Scooter

Large pillows or crash mat (see page 27 to make your own)

STEPS

1. Observe the actions your child is currently engaging in and note if something is affecting their ability to participate in a daily task, such as brushing their teeth.

2. Offer items/activities like the following as possibilities to assist with calming and organizing their body:

    • Sit and bounce on an exercise ball to help wake up, or push the ball around to get heavy work to the muscles to help calm the body.

    • Push/pull a laundry basket around the house to help calm the body.

    • Lie on a scooter and pull yourself with your arms to get heavy work to the shoulders and arms.

    • Jump on large pillows or a crash mat to get full-body input, or modify and wrap your child in stretchy or fluffy blankets.

3. Have your child try one of the activities in step 2, then have them complete the self-care or other task they were having trouble with, such as brushing their teeth.

To make it easier or harder: *As your child becomes more aware of their needs, provide them with choices, or let them independently choose activities to help calm and organize their body. See chapter 2 (beginning on page 21) for more activities based on various sensory systems.*

SKILLS
LEARNED

Memory

Planning and
Problem-Solving

Visual
Spatial Skills

Fine Motor
Skills

Matching Towers

Put on your hard hats and get ready to create identical block buildings! This activity works on visual memory and spatial skills, fine motor manipulation, and design skills.

Age: 2+
Prep time: 5 minutes
Activity time: 15 minutes

MATERIALS

Blocks (wood, Lego, etc.) in 3 different colors and sizes

STEPS

1. Design a 3-piece tower with 3 different colors or sizes of blocks.

2. Show the tower to your child and ask them to build the same tower.

3. Now design a 3-piece tower by starting with one colored piece or large piece at the bottom, a different color or smaller piece on top, and a piece of a different color or size next to the structure. Ask your child to create the same structure.

4. If any blocks are misplaced, help your child self-identify any errors with guiding questions:

    - "Are all the pieces in the right spot?"

    - "Do our buildings look the same?"

    If your child doesn't detect the error, ask questions that are more direct:

    - "It looks like your red block is on the bottom. Is that in the same space as my red block?"

    - "I placed my small block next to the big block. Where did you place your small block?"

To make it easier: *Have your child copy your building one block at a time.*

To make it harder: *Increase the number of blocks used with different shapes and colors and various locations, or use smaller blocks. Knock down your tower after building it and have your child build their copy from memory. Have your child lie in different positions as they work, such as on their belly or kneeling.*

SKILLS LEARNED	Attention	Memory	Planning and Problem-Solving

Schedule for Success

Create a visual schedule with steps, breaking down your child's self-care tasks such as brushing their teeth, washing their face, or toileting—or create a visual list of all the morning routines your child needs to complete. Visual schedules make it easier for children to remember the steps of a task and can reduce the need for constant reminders.

Age: 2+

Prep time: 30 minutes

Activity time: As long as needed

MATERIALS

Paper

Markers or crayons to draw pictures, or related images printed from the computer

Laminator and dry-erase marker (optional)

STEPS

1. Determine the list of tasks. For example, a list for brushing your teeth might look like this:

   ☐ Turn on the water at the sink.

   ☐ Place the toothbrush under the water.

   ☐ Turn off the water.

   ☐ Open the toothpaste.

   ☐ Squeeze a dot of toothpaste onto the toothbrush.

   ☐ Brush your bottom teeth for 1 minute.

   ☐ Brush your top teeth for 1 minute.

   ☐ Spit out the toothpaste.

   ☐ Turn on the water and rinse your toothbrush.

   ☐ Turn off the water.

   ☐ Put away the toothbrush and toothpaste.

2. Draw pictures that show the tasks.

3. Laminate the paper (if desired).

4. Review the list with your child before, during, and after the task to help them learn the skills (and to modify steps as needed). If the paper is laminated, use a dry-erase marker to check off steps as you go.

To make it easier: *Focus only on one or two simple tasks.*

To make it harder: *If your child is able to complete these routines, work on creating a list of all the tasks to complete in the morning, at night, or during any other daily routines..*

Find the Toy

Hide your child's favorite toy, then look for it as part of the game. Get creative with the directions you use to work on your child's visual searching skills, short-term and visual memory, planning, and problem-solving skills.

Age: 2+
Prep time: 1 to 2 minutes
Activity time: 15 minutes

MATERIALS

Child's favorite toy

STEPS

1. Have your child close their eyes and either count to 20 or wait for you to tell them they can open their eyes. While their eyes are closed, hide the toy in a place that will provide the appropriate level of challenge.

2. Provide verbal cues for location: getting close or far away, look up or down, look next to or under something, etc.

3. Take turns and let your child hide the toy and provide verbal directions to you.

To make it easier: *Hide the toy in an open space, or place the toy against objects of different colors.*

To make it harder: *Place the toy with objects of the same size, partially hidden, or in spaces that require problem-solving to reach for, such as under a small stool.*

Picture That

Mental rehearsal means thinking of images in your head and then planning actions. It can help kids learn daily routines or specific activities. The example below involves getting dressed, but you can swap in any task.

Age: 3+, depending on your child's communication abilities
Prep time: 2 minutes
Activity time: As needed to complete

MATERIALS

Pictures of the actions being described (optional)

STEPS

Ask your child guiding questions to help them "see" and mentally practice the activity. For example:

- "It's time to get ready for a cold snowy day. I wonder what clothes we need to get!"

- "You are now in your room. You look around and see your big brown dresser with the wooden knobs. You open the top drawer—what's inside?"

- "Yes! Now you pull on your long wool socks over your cold toes. Now what?"

- "You turn around to your closet and open it. What clothes do you see? You reach up for your warm red fleece pants, which you put your feet through and pull up."

- "Next, you reach up and pull your warmest sweater off the hanger. What color it is? What does it feel like when you pull it over your head?"

To make it easier: *Use pictures to help create a mental image in your child's head.*

To make it harder: *Have your child pick a task and describe it to you with as little or as much detail as you want.*

DIY Obstacle Course

Challenge cognitive, visual processing, and gross motor skills and encourage creativity by having your child create their own obstacle course based on the written or verbal descriptions you give them!

Age: 3+

Prep time: 15 to 20 minutes

Activity time: 15 to 20 minutes

MATERIALS

Paper (optional)

Pen or pencil (optional)

Household items a child can jump over, go under, and catch (jump rope, beanbag, etc.)

STEPS

1. Write directions for setting up an obstacle course. You can use verbal directions, too. For example: "Find something to jump over. Find something to go under. Find something to catch." Alternatively, draw a picture of a jump rope (to jump over), a picture of a broom on two chairs (to go under), and a beanbag (to catch).

2. Have your child figure out how to set up these items to create the obstacle course.

3. Have your child complete the obstacle course 4 or 5 times as you cheer them on!

To make it easier: *Provide verbal cues or directions for identifying and setting up objects, or for completing the course one step at a time.*

To make it harder: *Do the activity in a smaller space, where your child has to scan their surroundings and rely on their peripheral vision to navigate—but always consider safety. Have your child independently search for items within your home to build the obstacle course.*

Find the Treasure

Get out your pirate costumes! Here, you'll engage in an exciting treasure hunt. Your child will have so much fun they won't even realize they're honing skills such as direction following, visual searching, making logical connections, and creative thinking.

Age: 3+

Prep time: 15 to 30 minutes

Activity time: 15 to 30 minutes

MATERIALS

Index cards

Pencil or pen

Chosen object as the treasure, or a surprise

Play map and pirate costumes (optional)

STEPS

1. Write and hide the clues when your child is not looking. Make up your own, or use these suggestions:

    *   **Clue 1 (given to child):** Look at that, it's time for lunch! Where can you find some bread to munch? (Hide clue 2 in the pantry next to the bread.)

    *   **Clue 2:** Pee-yew, look at those feet! Where can you get them clean and neat? (Hide clue 3 in the bathtub.)

    *   **Clue 3:** Vroom-vroom, what's that sound? Four little wheels that are nice and round. (Hide clue 4 in a pile of toy cars.)

    *   **Clue 4:** If you brush for two minutes' time, your teeth will be rid of all their grime! (Hide clue 5 near the toothbrushes.)

    *   **Clue 5:** Hop, skip, dance, and jump—but you might need one for a scrape or bump. (Hide the treasure by the bandages or first-aid kit.)

2. Send your child to hunt for the clues. Read the clues out loud for younger kids but encourage them to think independently to find the next clue. Provide hints as needed, starting with broad suggestions and getting more specific if necessary.

To make it easier: *Go to various rooms and have your child find items based on categories, such as something round, something blue, or something small. Modify as needed, and get creative with favorite themes (such as a dinosaur fossil hunt, a princess adventure, etc.).*

To make it harder: *Have your child work with a sibling or friend. Increase the number of clues, or have your child come up with the clues and send you on the treasure hunt!*

Words-Only Obstacle Course

In this activity your child will take the lead and set up an obstacle course for you, describing the directions for you using only words—no demonstrations! This is a great activity for your child to work on body awareness, organizing thoughts, and sequencing and communicating ideas.

Age: 3+

Prep time: 15 minutes

Activity time: 30 minutes

MATERIALS

Home items good for crawling under, climbing over, stepping onto, balancing on, etc.

A tunnel, balance board, or stepping-stones (optional)

STEPS

1. Ask your child to identify which items they want to use. Have them set up the items in an obstacle course for you as you provide directions, if needed.

2. Ask your child to give you directions on how to complete the obstacle course, using only words. For example: "First, crawl through the tunnel. Second, jump over the stick with both feet."

3. Once you complete the course, have the child change the order and/or items and give you a new set of directions.

To make it easier: *If the child has a hard time describing with words, have them demonstrate the directions for you to follow.*

To make it harder: *Have a friend or sibling join, and work on coming up with ideas together or creating obstacle courses for each other.*

Spiderweb Maze

Using visual scanning skills and planning their body movements will help your child navigate through a large "spiderweb" maze on the ground. Don't get stuck in the web!

Age: 3+
Prep time: 20 minutes
Activity time: 10 to 15 minutes

MATERIALS

Chalk (if doing outdoors) or colored or plain masking or painter's tape

STEPS

1. Using chalk or tape, set up a maze on a large open surface, such as a kitchen floor or driveway, with clear starting and ending points. Start with a simple pathway with changes in direction, or try to replicate a more complex image from a coloring book.

2. Have your child start at the beginning and go through to the end, without crossing over the lines ("getting caught in the spiderweb").

To make it easier: *Keep it simple by just following a basic path.*

To make it harder: *Add motor and visual challenges. Invite your child to navigate by pushing an item such as a ball through the maze. Invite your child to make their own spiderweb maze and direct you through it.*

How High Can You Go?

Stack items as high as they'll go! Give your child instructions to build in all directions as they learn visual planning, organizing, and sequencing of ideas.

Age: 3+
Prep time: 2 minutes
Activity time: 15 minutes

MATERIALS

Wooden blocks, interconnecting blocks, large cardboard blocks, or other stackable items

STEPS

Give your child basic verbal directions to build something on a flat surface without visual aids. For example, say:

- "Build a tower as high as you can with the blocks."
- "See how high they can go without falling down."
- "You can build up, down, to the side, and to the front and back."
- "Take your time. Fit as many blocks as you can on the table."

To make it easier: *Have your child just build a vertical tower. Set a limit on the number of blocks used.*

To make it harder: *Have your child verbally describe how to build the tower without physically doing it. Ask guiding questions to help your child determine if their idea will work or not.*

I'd Like to Order a Sandwich

Have your child practice following directions and using memory skills by placing an order using play food items. The example here uses a sandwich but feel free to use any play food you like.

Age: 3+

Prep time: 5 minutes

Activity time: 20 minutes

MATERIALS

Pretend play food items, such as pieces of a sandwich-stacking game or pretend pizza pieces

Pretend play utensils (optional)

Menu (optional)

Dress-up clothing (optional)

STEPS

1. Set up the play food items across the room, away from the "eating" area.

2. Sit down at the eating area and order food from your child. Start off with one or two requests and build on them as your child succeeds. For example:

   - "May I please have a sandwich with bread and turkey?"

   - "I would like to order a sandwich with turkey and pickles." (The child has to remember that a sandwich contains bread.)

   - "I'm really hungry! How about a sandwich with turkey, cheese, tomatoes, lettuce, and pickles?"

3. Review the order when your child brings you the sandwich to reflect on their creation. Thank them for their good service!

To make it easier: *To help with memory, provide pictures of the items wanted on the sandwich.*

To make it harder: *Change your mind after you place an order and ask for something else instead.*

Moving Hoops

Who doesn't love a moving target? In this game, your child will work on hand-eye coordination, visual tracking, and planning skills by trying to throw an item through a moving target. Use a Hula-Hoop, a bucket, or even an upside-down traffic cone and move it around as your child tries to aim for the target.

Age: 4+

Prep time: 5 minutes

Activity time: 15 minutes

MATERIALS

A target: Hula-Hoop, bucket, etc.

Something to throw: ball, beanbag, stuffed animal

Balance board or an uneven surface to stand on (optional)

STEPS

1. Stand across from your child in a large safe area, indoors or out.

2. While standing still, slowly move the target side to side or back and forth.

3. Cheer your child on as you tell them where to throw ("Higher!" "Lower!" "Behind me!"). Move the target more or less, depending on their success rate.

4. As they progress, slowly widen the range of the target.

5. Have your child follow you as you move around with the target.

To make it easier: *Verbally state the direction you're moving in, or move the target toward where they are throwing.*

To make it harder: *Use a smaller ball or smaller target to improve hand-eye coordination, or add additional motor challenges, such as having them stand on a balance board or on one leg while throwing.*

Musical Mats

With its use of different categories and colored mats, this movement game is a fun way to practice memory, visual searching, and listening to and following directions. Include some background music as a way for your child to work through background noise and learn to filter additional input.

Age: 4+
Prep time: 20 minutes
Activity time: 15 minutes

MATERIALS

9 pieces of colored paper (3 sets of 3 different colors)

Markers, or images from magazines or online

Scissors (if using print-outs or magazines)

Glue sticks (if using printouts or magazines)

Laminator (optional)

Background music of choice, on low volume

STEPS

1. Have your child identify which 3 colors of paper to use for the 9 mats. Let's say they choose green, red, and yellow.

2. Have your child think of 3 animals, shapes, toys, or other items. Let's say they choose a triangle, circle, and square.

3. Draw a triangle or glue a picture of a triangle on each color of paper, so you have one green mat with a triangle, one red mat with a triangle, and one yellow mat with a triangle. Repeat the process with the other two shapes. These are your movement mats.

4. Laminate the mats, if desired.

5. Spread out the movement mats on a flat surface and turn on the music.

6. Start by calling out a color or category for your child to walk over to. For example, say, "Green." The child can go to any green mat. Then say, "Circle." The child can then go to any mat with a circle on it.

7. Increase the challenge by calling a color and category together—for example, "green triangle" or "red circle"—so there's only one possible mat for your child to walk to.

To make it easier: *Turn off the music.*

To make it harder: *Speed up the game, or add different positions to navigate between the mats such as a bear walk, crab walk, or snake crawl.*

SKILLS LEARNED	Attention	Memory	Planning and Problem-Solving	Self-Awareness	Gross Motor Skills

Ready, Set ... Stop or Go?

Get ready . . . get set . . . wait for the directions! Work on your child's ability to wait and follow through with directions, coordinate their body, be safe, and quickly shift their attention to new directions. Will your child keep their balance, stop what they're doing, or start a new task when directions are given?

Age: 4+

Prep time: 20 minutes

Activity time: 15 minutes

MATERIALS

Obstacle course (see DIY Obstacle Course [page 150] or Words-Only Obstacle Course [page 154] for ideas), Moving Hoops (page 158), or get creative with a new activity

1 green piece of paper or green marker

1 red piece of paper or red marker

Additional paper and marker (optional)

STEPS

1. Set up the desired activity (Obstacle Course, Moving Hoops, etc.).

2. Have your child start the activity. As they go, tell them you will hold up your red paper or marker to indicate "stop" and green paper or marker to indicate "go." Red means they should stop doing the activity; green means they can go back to doing the activity. When you signal stop or go, see how long it takes your child to respond and make the challenge easier or harder accordingly.

3. Vary the activity by adding other written, visual, or verbal directions, such as "Move on to the next step," "Go back to the last step," or "Add a new step"—such as different animal walks.

To make it easier: *Begin with stop and go messages at the clear beginning or end of an action and slowly work toward using them in the middle of an action.*

To make it harder: *Use only verbal directions to address auditory processing while engaging in a movement task. Call out non-relevant/funny words instead of "stop" or "go" to help your child build on listening and safety-awareness skills.*

Attention	Memory	Planning and Problem-Solving	Shared Engagement	Communication	Play Development	SKILLS LEARNED

Lights, Camera, Action

With your guidance, let your child make their own story to build on, connecting play ideas and understanding the perspectives of others.

Age: 5+
Prep time: 10 minutes
Activity time: 30 minutes

MATERIALS

Dress-up clothes

Any items associated with the chosen theme (optional)

STEPS

1. Let your child pick the topic for a play, such as saving a prince from a castle or rescuing people who've been shipwrecked.

2. Your child is the director. Let them assign roles, direct actions, describe characters' emotions, and set up play items/props.

3. The adult's role is to guide the child through the process as needed. Some things to consider:

   - Is the child thinking ahead and planning ideas to sequence play components?

   - Are the ideas being logically connected so an "outsider" could follow the "plot"?

   - Can your child answer questions to help further describe the play "story"?

4. Give the child enough time to work through the process using trial and error, providing support as needed to bring their theatrical vision to life!

To make it easier: *Break down the activity to work on just one component of the play idea. For example, instead of saving everyone from a shipwreck, just focus on navigating the boat.*

To make it harder: *For older kids, add a writing activity by encouraging them to create a script, or create the play with only imaginary props.*

I Have a Different Idea!

This is where creativity meets flexible thinking! As your child creates elaborate pretend play scenes, another point of view (yours) will come onto the scene. Are you thinking something different? How can your child work together with someone who changes their play idea?

Age: 5+

Prep time: 10 minutes

Activity time: 30 minutes

MATERIALS

Dress-up clothes

Any items associated with the chosen theme (optional)

STEPS

1. Let your child pick the idea/topic, such as pirates, princesses, or jungle animals, and encourage them to create a story line that logically connects ideas.

2. As you're playing, introduce a completely different or "wacky" concept (whether that means fighting off a castle invasion, making the animals talk, or pretending it's raining tacos).

3. Give your child time to think and wait for a response. Provide support for any emotional response and talk about feelings as needed.

4. Encourage your child to allow this "change" or difference in ideas. Talk about rationale and feelings. For example, if you ask your child why they chose to wear the princess dress and how it makes them feel, they may say, "I picked the princess dress because it makes me feel pretty." Ask them why others might have chosen a different outfit. How does that make your child feel?

5. If there are differences in opinion, make adjustments and work together toward a solution or compromise.

To make it easier: *Your child may not be ready to participate in this activity, and that's okay! Discuss feelings in the moment and how or why the activity is hard, such as stating, "It looks like you might be feeling sad or frustrated because you wanted a turn as the superhero and I went first."*

To make it harder: *Once this is mastered with an adult, have siblings or peers join to work toward cooperative/organized group play.*

Dough Chef

Pull out your chef's aprons and make some play dough as your child works on following directions, visual searching and discrimination skills, keeping an organized workspace, and kitchen safety.

Age: 5+, with assistance for reading as needed
Prep time: 10 to 20 minutes
Activity time: 10 minutes

MATERIALS

Typed directions or images

Dry and wet measuring cups

All-purpose flour (gluten-free if needed)

Large bowl

Salt

Measuring spoons

Cream of tartar

Large spoon

Warm water

Food coloring

Airtight container or resealable bag

STEPS

1. Put all the ingredients and equipment in a box or on a table.

2. Provide your child with written and/or visual directions of the following recipe:

   - Put 1 cup of flour in a bowl.
   - Add ¼ cup of salt to the bowl.
   - Add 1 tablespoon cream of tartar to the bowl.
   - Stir together and set aside.
   - Measure ½ cup of warm water.
   - Add 5 drops of food coloring to the water and stir.
   - Slowly pour the water into the flour mixture, stirring as you pour.
   - Use your hands to knead the flour to make a ball of play dough. If it's too sticky, add more flour.
   - Store in an airtight container or resealable bag.

3. As your child follows the recipe, provide cues as needed, starting broadly and becoming more specific if necessary.

4. Observe how your child organizes and keeps the work space clean or cluttered, how easily they find and measure items, and whether they miss any recipe steps. Offer help when needed.

To make it easier: *Provide the necessary measuring items at each step.*

To make it harder: *Present the items in a disorganized fashion so your child can work on visual scanning. You could also add an extra item or leave one out so your child can work on problem-solving such as omitting the unnecessary item or searching in the kitchen for the missing item.*

What Comes Next?

I hope you find these activities beneficial for your child and that they work well in conjunction with the approaches used in their occupational therapy sessions.

Continue to use as many or as few activities as you like, monitoring how your child performs and watching for fatigue as well as motivation for continued engagement. If your child is not currently receiving occupational therapy services and you think they may benefit, please follow up with your primary care physician and see which services are available in your area based on your child's age and needs.

Some children require occupational therapy through childhood and well into adolescence. As children get older, occupational therapy intervention shifts from focusing on play to focusing on daily life routines, including self-care, house management, and community living skills. Interventions may also shift from working toward specific developmental milestones to making adaptations and modifications to your child's routine and surroundings in order for them to achieve the greatest amount of success. Relationship-based approaches and family-centered care are still integral to a young adult's treatment, but now the goal is for them to be as independent as possible and an active member of their community, no matter how much or what kind of support they need.

The important thing for parents and caregivers to know is that every skill you take the time to provide your child with now is one more tool they'll have to help them navigate and effectively handle whatever circumstances, opportunities, and challenges present themselves in the future.

Resources

- - - - - - - - - - - - -

SOCIAL-EMOTIONAL DEVELOPMENT, RELATIONSHIP BUILDING, AND PLAY APPROACHES

DIRFloortime

The Interdisciplinary Council on Development and Learning: www.icdl.com/dir/

Parent-Friendly DIR website: www.affectautism.com/

Engaging Autism: Using the Floortime Approach to Help Children Relate, Communicate, and Think by Stanley Greenspan and Serena Wieder

MINDFULNESS APPROACHES

Mindsight Institute, work of Dr. Dan Siegel: www.drdansiegel.com/books_and_more/

SENSORY PROCESSING

Resources on interoception: www.kelly-mahler.com/resources/

Sensational Kids: Hope and Help for Children with Sensory Processing Disorder (SPD) by Lucy Jane Miller

STAR Institute for Sensory Processing Disorder: www.spdstar.org/

The Out-of-Sync Child: Recognizing and Coping with Sensory Processing Disorder by Carol Kranowitz

References

Case-Smith, Jane, and Jane Clifford O'Brien, eds. *Occupational Therapy for Children*. Maryland Heights, MO: Mosby Elsevier.

Centers for Disease Control and Prevention. "Diagnostic Criteria for 299.00 Autism Spectrum Disorder." Accessed October 11, 2019. https://www.cdc.gov/ncbddd /autism/hcp-dsm.html.

Interdisciplinary Council on Development and Learning. "Functional Emotional Developmental Capacities (FEDCs)." Accessed October 11, 2019. https://www.icdl .com/dir/fedcs.

Mayo Clinic. "Cerebral Palsy." Accessed October 11, 2019. https://www.mayoclinic .org/diseases-conditions/cerebral-palsy/symptoms-causes/syc-20353999.

National Autistic Society. "Autism." Accessed October 11, 2019. https://www.autism .org.uk/about/what-is/asd.aspx.

STAR Institute for Sensory Processing Disorder. "Subtypes of SPD." Accessed October 11, 2019. https://www.spdstar.org/basic/subtypes-of-spd.

STAR Institute for Sensory Processing Disorder. "Understanding Sensory Processing Disorder." Accessed October 11, 2019. https://www.spdstar.org/basic /understanding-sensory-processing-disorder.

US Department of Education. "About IDEA." Accessed October 11, 2019. https:// sites.ed.gov/idea/about-idea.

Yamkovenko, Stephanie. "The Role of OT with Persons with Down Syndrome." Accessed October 11, 2019. https://www.aota.org/about-occupational-therapy /professionals/cy/articles/down.aspx.

Index

Acknowledgments

Thank you to my husband, Andrei, who continues to support and push me to reach for my dreams when working with children and families in occupational therapy sessions. I also would like to thank my colleague Danielle Otieno, OTR/L, who is constantly available to bounce ideas off of both for this book and for practical use during therapy sessions. Her creativity and unique treatment skills are invaluable.

About the Author

Dr. Heather Ajzenman, OTD, OTR/L, HPCS, received her doctorate in occupational therapy from Washington University in Saint Louis in 2012. She is a DIRFloortime Advanced Certified Provider and a hippotherapy clinical specialist (HPCS). She has experience working with diverse families and children from birth to 21 years of age using a family-centered, evidence-based approach. She currently sits on the Scientific Advisory Council for the Horses and Humans Research Foundation, previously served on the board of directors for the American Hippotherapy Association, and has published research on hippotherapy in the *American Journal of Occupational Therapy*. She lives in New Hampshire with her husband, daughter, dog, horse, and other animals.

Printed in the USA
CPSIA information can be obtained
at www.ICGtesting.com
CBHW042103220524
8965CB00002B/4